P9-CEZ-223

To Vietnam with Love

To Vietnam with Love

THE STORY OF
CHARLIE AND EG LONG

Charles E. Long

Christian Publications
CAMP HILL, PENNSYLVANIA

Christian Publications
3825 Hartzdale Drive, Camp Hill, PA 17011

Faithful, biblical publishing since 1883

ISBN: 0-87509-582-8
LOC Catalog Card Number: 94-80026
© 1995 by Christian Publications
All rights reserved
Printed in the United States of America

95 96 97 98 99   5 4 3 2 1

Cover Illustration
© 1995 by Karl Foster

Unless otherwise indicated, Scripture taken from the
HOLY BIBLE: NEW INTERNATIONAL VERSION ®.
© 1973, 1978, 1984 by the International Bible Society.
Used by permission of Zondervan Publishing House.
All rights reserved.

First Dedication

We dedicate this book to
Four Little Missionaries—

John Nathan
Robert Edward
Amelia Susan
and *Joanna Elizabeth*

who were not in Vietnam by choice—
they were born there.
Just their presence opened doors for us,
gave us credibility with the Vietnamese,
softened the hearts of mean people,
gave joy to U.S. servicemen.
They took great risks without
fully understanding the consequences.

John Nathan
A very suntanned Nathan once said, "Dad,
they'll think I am a little Jarai boy." I looked into
his bright blue eyes and said, "I don't think so, son.
Your eyes are different."

Robert Edward
We had just missed an ambush involving a 110-
truck convoy, but we were still 55 kilometers from

Pleiku. We took the risk of returning behind three ARVN trucks. "If they shoot," I told six-year-old Eddie, "I'll stop the car. As soon as it stops, you jump in the ditch and stay down on your tummy until I myself call you, okay?" Steady Eddie said, "Okay, Daddy."

Amelia Susan
Susie had a smile that disarmed the most contrary adults we encountered. Her little-girl charm made many soldiers homesick for their families.

Joanna Elizabeth
All our children prayed for us and for "the translation," but it was Joby who lived closest to us while we worked to finish it. I remember her delight to see me hand the finished work to the United Bible Society staff in Hong Kong on July 4, 1974.

Thank you,
Nathan
Eddie
Susie
and Joby.

We love you with all our hearts.
You helped us love Vietnam!

Charlie and EG, your dad and mom

Second Dedication

This book is dedicated to

The Little Denomination That Does—

The Christian and Missionary Alliance.

By this story we honor the faithful visionary pastor
and faithful lay people who
give, pray and inspire young people to go
to all nations with the Good News of
Our Lord Jesus Christ.

This book salutes:

Rev. Homer P. Williams

and the thousands of pastors like him
who have denied themselves to send missionaries
to the millions of the many lands of
The Christian and Missionary Alliance
over the past more than 100 years.
We have sown together
and the harvest is ours.

EG and I humbly thank and admire
the many visionary men and women, boys and girls

who made Faith Promises and gave the funds
that gave us the freedom
to pour out our lives in Vietnam.
Tens of thousands of Jarai will hug and kiss you
in heaven!
We have sown together
and the harvest is ours.

At the close of our 18 years of service as missionaries in 1976, I spoke at the First Alliance Church in Winston-Salem, North Carolina. As I walked down the aisle toward the rear of the sanctuary, a little gray-haired lady approached me. She showed me a worn, yellowed, dog-eared copy of the prayer reminder card of a very young couple who went to Vietnam as missionaries in 1958.
"I have prayed for you every day since I received this card," she said.
I weep for joy at that service to Christ!

We of The Christian and Missionary Alliance
have sown together and the harvest is ours.

To God be the glory
for
the Little Denomination That Does!

Contents

Acknowledgments

To the hundreds of people who have taught us, prayed for us, encouraged us and funded us—

We are forever indebted. Though you are not listed here, you know who you are! Thank you.

To the missionaries who were our "Seniors" in Vietnam—

Thank you for welcoming us to the ministry not as inferior "Juniors" but as much appreciated help and as valued co-workers. You were great examples, teachers and role models. Thank you for being Christlike!

To Rev. and Mrs. Truong van Sang, our closest co-workers among the Jarai at Pleiku—

Thank you for being our cultural guides through our many blunders in your home country. You served steadfastly till the end. Your reward surely is great.

To Rev. and Mrs. David A. Frazier and Rev. and Mrs. Gail Fleming—

Thank you for every minute of fellowship, education, encouragement, car repair, chess matches, advice, laughter, pain, help and blessing. I still can't speak any Bahnar! Did ya'll ever learn any Jarai? I wish we could do it all over again only BETTER!

To our predecessors at Pleiku,
Rev. and Mrs. T. Grady Mangham and
Rev. and Mrs. Walter Eugene Evans—

Thank you for the foundation laid for anything that happened later among the Jarai. You must be the ones who began their singing tradition. They are still the greatest singers!

To our parents Joe and Eunice Long and
Elma Baldwin Davis—

Thank you for your unwavering support. You let us "crazy" people bring up four of your grandchildren in the madness of the Vietnam war without ever a hint that we should turn back. Thank you!

To Rev. Robert Cowles—

Thank you for your desire to see this story told and for pressing on until it has become a reality. May all who read this compressed story of our 18 years as missionaries be moved to answer "yes" to the voice of Jesus Christ saying, "Follow Me!"

1

"Bad Dads from Baghdad"

For weeks my friend Bob Robertson had begged me to date EG. Each time I turned him down.

It was 1953. I was planning that fall to enter the University of North Carolina, Charlotte. I lived in Charlotte and the university had offered me a scholarship. I wanted to go with no strings attached. Besides, who was EG?

My friend Bob and I went all the way back to first grade. We were chosen from our grammar school to sing in the Charlotte Boys' Choir sponsored by the local Rotary Club. From age 10 to 14 we sang for the Rotary from the Carolinas to New York City (Madison Square Garden, no less) to Daytona Beach, Florida.

Bob had raven black hair that curled into ringlets. That made him perfectly suited to be dressed as an 1890s girl, complete with long skirt and parasol, for one of our choir numbers. It was a great act but it made Bob super-sensitive about being called a girl. More than one fellow got "five in the mouth" for teasing Bob about his hair or calling him a sissy.

Since I had no brothers, Bob and his brother Bill were very important to my survival on Charlotte's tough "macho" streets. To call someone chicken on those streets often led to rooster-like fist fights. I hated it, but I also learned to fight.

Bob and I were in the eleventh grade when he received Jesus Christ into his life. Relentlessly Bob began talking to me about Jesus and, just as stubbornly, I dodged him. But knowing how much I enjoyed singing, Bob managed to rope me into singing bass in a Youth for Christ quartette. Words such as "I once was lost in sin/But Jesus took me in" convicted me. I was embarrassed to sing something I did not mean.

But back to EG.

The initials, I was to learn later, stood for Elma Grace—Elma Grace Davis. EG had grown up in the little town of McDonald, North Carolina. She was raised a Presbyterian but during her growing-up years she had attended a service at McDonald's Baptist Church where two Christian and Missionary Alliance missionaries told of their work in West Africa. That night EG began to answer the call of God to be a missionary.

Now in 1953 she was in Charlotte in further pursuit of that call, studying nursing at Presbyterian Hospital. She and other nursing students attended Calvary Presbyterian Church across the street from the hospital and also participated in the Saturday night Youth for Christ rallies at Central High Auditorium—which was how Bob got to know them.

August 1953 arrived and with it decision time for me. Many of my buddies had gone to war in Korea. Others joined the Air National Guard and began to train as fighter pilots. I went to enroll for college as planned but I simply could not sign up. In spite of the scholarship, I was not settled enough to make a commitment.

Bob pestered me again about EG. He had arranged a date with Kay, another of the student nurses.

"Come on, Long," he urged, "let's double-date Friday night. EG and Kay are going to be babysitting one of the nurses' kids."

"Do they have TV?" I asked. (Television sets were not yet commonplace.) "I want to watch the football game."

"I think so," was Bob's half-encouraging reply.

So it was, on Friday night, August 7, 1953, that three really great love stories began.

The first was very obvious. I met the most beautiful, slightly-freckled, sparkling-eyed, quiet-spoken girl God ever made. I have yet to recover from that day.

The second love story began the next night, August 8, 1953, when, convicted by the Christ I saw living in EG and under a heavy cloud of real guilt for real sin, I asked Jesus to save me.

I remember the scene as if it were yesterday.

Bob and I were parked in front of Bob's house in my Dad's 1951 Chevy. Bob had been talking to me about the Lord for an hour or more. I kept responding that all my past effort to reform had failed. Bob told me I needed "to ask for a miracle."

I knew deep down in my heart that he was right. A miracle was exactly what I needed. Finally, I simply bowed my head over the steering wheel and surrendered to Jesus Christ. I went home not knowing all the implications of that decision.

The next day I woke up clean, forgiven, made new by the most gracious Person in the universe. He loved me and His love taught me to love. Saturday night the crushing load of my sins against God had felt like a 20,000-foot-high mountain piled on my chest. Sunday morning when I awoke I felt so free of the weight that it was like flying 20,000 feet above the earth. I began to believe that what God had done for me overnight, He could do for any poor sinner.

A passion began to grow in my heart to tell the world about it—especially people far away from churches, radios and the readily available gospel that was so commonplace in the USA.

I had to be a missionary! Who? Me? How? Me?

Yes, me. I would see to it that some untouched language group would have John 1:12 to read and experience: " . . . to all who received him, to those who believed in his name, he gave the right to become children of God."

The third love story. . . . Well, I am getting ahead of myself. That will have to wait until later.

✦ ✦ ✦

Charlie Boyd, a Youth for Christ friend in Charlotte, drove Bob and me in search of a college that taught Bible. We "happened" on Toccoa Falls Col-

lege, southwest of Charlotte in the piney woods of
north Georgia, a school affiliated with The Christian and Missionary Alliance.

From the open window of the college registrar's
office I could hear a creek bubbling. It seemed to
be saying, "This is the place to be alone with God
and get it all together."

Less than three weeks later my dad delivered Bob
and me to Morrison Hall on the Toccoa Falls campus. The creek that flowed near the registrar's office also flowed by Morrison Hall. I could hear its
bubbling from my dorm window. Its message was
unchanged. I felt reassured that I was where God
wanted me to be.

Bob and I arrived on campus with duck-tail hair-
cuts, pegged pants—complete with narrow cuffs,
wide knees, wide seams and pistol flaps on the
pockets—shirt collars turned up, and chips on our
shoulders. Years later an upper classman would tell
me he thought we would be "shipped" within a
week!

In Charlotte we had been known as the "bad
dads from Baghdad—too bad to be had, too mean
to be seen and too cool to be ruled." Now here I
was in love with Jesus Christ and eager to study
His truth.

Thankfully, at least some of the college staff
could see past my wild and crazy facade to the
grace of God working within. They tolerated me
until God in His love could do His refining work.

It is a process still ongoing.

Every month, come rain or shine, sleet or snow, I
hitchhiked from the college to Charlotte in pursuit

of EG. In the fall the rolling hills were clad in multi-colored leaves, in winter in white snow, in spring in pink peach blossoms. I was in love and I was alive to everything.

EG was hard to get. She graduated from her training and began to work as a nurse. I continued to pursue her. Then, in the summer of 1955, almost two years after our first meeting, she shocked me by agreeing to marry me.

That fall we went together to Toccoa Falls College. I played basketball and EG and I sang in the college choir. Among other subjects, I took Greek and high school Latin. That was because I had failed Latin in high school.

But here I was planning to be a missionary. How could I face learning another language? Did I dare say that I wanted to translate the Bible into another language? I, who had failed high school Latin? The thought of failing sent goose bumps over my zeal. I knew in my heart that I had to face and defeat the language monster or give up the idea of being a missionary.

When I passed both courses with good grades, I finally began to believe I could learn a language, be a missionary and even be what I considered to be the elite of missionaries—a Bible translator.

In addition to our studies and singing in the choir, EG and I both worked. We loved school, we loved living and we loved each other.

With our sights set on overseas ministry, my heroes now were missionaries. I followed the stories of the five young men martyred by the Aucas in Ecuador. And I was especially drawn to

the Alliance missionaries pioneering in Irian Jaya—
Mickelson, Lewis, Rose, Van Stone, Bromley,
Bozeman, Catto.

So EG and I studied the country of New Guinea,
as Irian Jaya was then called, in preparation for
working among the tribespeople there. I was six
feet four inches tall, young and in excellent health.
I figured it was my duty to take on the toughest
mission assignment. And right then, New Guinea
was it.

We graduated from Toccoa in 1957 and headed
to the Summer Institute of Linguistics at the
University of Oklahoma. It was there we met Rev.
Orman Knight of the Tabernacle Baptist Church of
Chicago. That fall he saw our names on the roster
at Missionary Internship and asked for us to be assigned as interns to his church.

The Tab, as we called it, sent us to the western
suburbs of the city to start a new church. It was
hard. I learned to deal with rejection when people
slammed doors in my face. I also learned to boldly
ask people about their relationship with Jesus
Christ.

And another thing—Chicago was a foreign land!
I was from the south and was unmercifully, even
cruelly, teased about my southern drawl.

In spite of it all, by May of 1958, we had assembled a group of about 50 people, some of them
new Christians, into what became the First Baptist
Church of Villa Park.

While we were in Chicago we received a life-
changing letter from our Christian and Missionary
Alliance national office. We were being asked to go

to Vietnam.

Vietnam? Where was that? That was before Vietnam had become a household word in America. I went to the library to locate it in an atlas. I found it listed under French Indo-China, a small country nestled beneath the mass of Communist China. I had followed the Korean War with interest and remembered seeing the hordes of Chinese troops swarming over the hills.

Are you sure about this, Lord? I prayed mentally. *I don't want to die just because I am an American. I am ready to give my life for You but not for the sake of politics.*

God used a strange Scripture verse from Isaiah to reassure me. In the King James Version it reads, "Sanctify the LORD of hosts himself; and let him be your fear, and let him be your dread" (8:13). To me God was saying: "Never fear any man. Only fear that you will fail Me."

It was the word I needed then and it proved to be the word for all our years in Vietnam: "Sanctify the LORD of hosts himself; and let him be your fear, and let him be your dread."

We completed our internship in Chicago, proceeded to Canada for a month-long course at the Toronto Institute of Linguistics and returned to Charlotte to finish our packing and say our good-byes.

On Tuesday, August 12, 1958, EG, six months pregnant, and I flew to San Francisco where we boarded a propeller-driven Pan American Stratocruiser for the hopscotch Pacific crossing—Honolulu, Wake Island, Guam, Manila and finally,

Saigon.

Each eight- or nine-hour leg of the flight seemed endless, the four spinning propellers appearing motionless, painted between blue sky and blue water. Only the steady drone of the motors testified to our progress.

It was Saturday, August 16 when we touched down to the sights, sounds, smells and heat of Saigon. No classroom could possibly have prepared us for the reality. I cannot begin to describe the excitement, the curiosity, the expectation, the joy, the fun we felt at that moment.

It was the first day of the rest of our lives. We had finally arrived where God wanted us to be.

2

Vietnam

Vietnam, as Americans are painfully aware, is where our country fought a very unpopular war. Not since the Civil War a century earlier had the nation been so divided. It was a war begun with high hopes of freedom and security for South Vietnam.

But by the end of the 1960s many Americans thought the United States had no business being there. They began to believe Vietnam was of little strategic value to America. They gave up trying to defend it against the communist juggernaut backed by China and the Soviet Union. Defending it was costing American lives.

Missionaries in Vietnam had a different perspective. There was a combined population in South Vietnam and its neighbors, Laos and Cambodia, of more than 28 million. Most of them still needed to hear the good news about Jesus.

Until the war made Vietnam a household word and brought Southeast Asia to international prominence, The Christian and Missionary Alliance was the only Protestant Mission establishing churches in all three countries.

In Vietnam, North and South, these churches had the name *Tin Lanh* (Teen LAAN)—*Tin* meaning "news" and *Lanh,* "good"—Good News Churches.

The missionaries knew the attitude of the communists toward God and Christianity. If Southeast Asia fell to these anti-Christian aggressors it would mean the end of missionary activity and the beginning of a long night for the Church of Jesus Christ in Southeast Asia.

As it turned out, all of us were partly wrong. The anti-war people, who persuaded America to abandon Southeast Asia to the communists, have the blood of a million Cambodians and hundreds of thousands of South Vietnamese and Laotians on their consciences. And we, who supposed a communist take-over would be the end of evangelistic work there, did not know all that God was intending to do. He would not only preserve His church but greatly expand it.

But that's getting ahead of my story.

When EG and I landed on Vietnamese soil on August 16, 1958, Alliance missionaries had already been there 47 years. In fact, as early as 1882, Albert B. Simpson, founder of The Christian and Missionary Alliance, had looked compassionately at the Indo-China peninsula. It was one of many world areas where the good news of Jesus Christ had yet to reach. He prayed that some of the young men and women enrolled in his New York City Missionary Training Institute would change that situation.

In July 1891 there was an explosion of missionary recruits. Two years later, A.B. Simpson made a round-the-world trip to be sure the more than 200 fledgling missionaries, many with less than one year of training, were properly directed and doing acceptable work.

One of his scouts was David LeLacheur, who passed through Vietnam, then called Annam, on his way to Singapore to report to Dr. Simpson. He urged Simpson to consider sending missionaries to Annam. But Simpson had neither the personnel nor the dollars to invest in another operation.

Eight more years passed.

On January 12, 1896, as Robert A. Jaffray, a Canadian and the namesake of this series, farewelled the Gospel Tabernacle in New York, he appealed at length for missionaries to Annam.

Later that year, Clarence Reeves, a South China missionary, traveled to Annam. He died there of smallpox in 1898.

Robert Jaffray took Reeves' place, arriving in Hanoi on February 10, 1899.

Back in Canada a year later, Jaffray persuaded Mr. and Mrs. Sylvan Dayan, a French Canadian couple, to enter the area. Jaffray was confident they would find favor with the French, then the overseers of Annam. The Dayans' efforts to establish a beachhead were unsuccessful and they returned home in 1904.

But Jaffray refused to let his vision die. Almost a decade later, in 1911, together with fellow missionaries Lloyd Hughes and Paul Hosler, he spearheaded the first permanent Protestant incursion into Vietnam.

They entered Tourane, the port city the Vietnamese call Danang (Daa NAANG). Although Jaffray himself never established a residence in Vietnam and Hughes did not live long, the beachhead in Danang held. Nourished by new personnel, the missionary front in Indo-China began to expand.

The First World War threatened the well-being of the operation. The French overlords expelled two missionaries, including Hosler, and forbade the remaining ones to preach or to travel beyond the limits of Tourane.

No matter. People came in from the countryside, heard the gospel, believed in Christ and began churches. The French, impressed by the exemplary morality of the believers, soon relaxed their restrictions on the missionaries.

From its beginning in 1911 through World War II, the Alliance was the only Protestant Mission establishing churches in Vietnam. The politically tumultuous years following the war were especially difficult for the church. Ho Chi Minh (Ho Chee MEN), the Marxist-Leninist leader of a relatively small nationalist movement within Vietnam, had been fighting the Japanese. When Japan surrendered to the Allies, Ho Chi Minh and his Viet Minh were left in de facto control of much of northern and central Vietnam.

Despite U.S. opposition and local opinion, the British returned Indo-China to the French. Meanwhile, the Viet Minh served notice that all of Vietnam was under the leadership of Ho Chi Minh.

The First Vietnam War was underway.

A short-lived truce between the French and the

Viet Minh lasted only long enough for the French to gain control of Hanoi and other urban areas in both the north and south. Ho Chi Minh and his forces retreated to the hills, where they were reinforced by weaponry and other supplies from Communist China just across the border.

During those years of French/Vietnamese infighting, scores of churches were destroyed, rebuilt and destroyed again and again. Dozens of pastors and hundreds of church members were murdered and thousands more jailed and otherwise exiled.

French efforts against the insurgents went from bad to worse, loosening their grip on Indo-China. In the celebrated battle at Dien Bien Phu (Dee-ONG Bee-ONG FOO), the Viet Minh forces vanquished the remaining French control in Southeast Asia.

Vietnam was partitioned at the 17th parallel pending national elections. The elections were never held. The partitioning made North Vietnam off limits to all Western missionaries, in fact, to any missionaries.

Not so the South. Alliance leaders, recognizing the window of opportunity God was providing, pushed as much personnel as possible through the opening. Some would be assigned to the 16 million Vietnamese living along the narrow coast of South Vietnam and in the fertile delta below Saigon. Yet others would be sent to the dozens of tribes, some very large, occupying the mountain jungles that stretched like a massive spinal column from the demilitarized zone (DMZ) southward.

For the most part, these estimated 1.2 million

tribespeople were yet unevangelized. A major obstacle was the difficulty of communication. Each tribe had its own language or dialect and relatively few spoke or even understood Vietnamese.

Efforts by earlier missionaries, beginning in 1929, had found the populace responsive. A handful of Tin Lanh (National Church) missionaries joined those from overseas. Their joint ministry resulted in several thousand professing believers.

The wave of new missionary appointees reached its crescendo from 1956 to 1959. EG and I were among them, arriving in August, 1958. We were very young, very inexperienced and very naive, but very sure of God's call to Vietnam.

3

Good Times, Bad Times

A long with other arriving new missionaries, EG and I were sent to Danang to learn Vietnamese. In all, there were 27 fledgling missionaries under the tutelage of George and Harriette Irwin. George and Harriette had both grown up in Vietnam and spoke Vietnamese fluently.

George could also eat red peppers and *nuoc mam* (noo-uk MAAM) like a Vietnamese. (*Nuoc mam* is a clear, tea-colored liquid tapped from large wooden vats after tiny fish, aged in brine, have disintegrated. It is the Vietnamese seasoning of choice for most dishes.)

George was not only in charge of language study at Danang but he also worked as a district missionary, making extensive week-long forays into all the northern region of South Vietnam.

To give the new missionaries a taste of what it was like to be out there among the tribespeople, he would take one of the male missionaries with him on each trip.

My turn came about three months after our arrival. I hadn't yet gotten used to chopsticks, I didn't know much Vietnamese and I certainly knew none of the tribal dialects. But George and I, along with Rev. Loc (LAWP), drove north and west up toward the Vietnamese/Laotian border to spend a week with the Bru (BROO) tribespeople.

It turned out to be quite a trip.

When we had gone as far as possible by Jeep, we shouldered our hefty pack baskets and set out on foot through the tall savannah grass. This was tiger country!

We were escorted from one location to another by villagers who would remark, "My grandmother was killed there," or "My uncle was killed over there," as they pointed out the places where the incidents had taken place. One village alone reported a total of 70 deaths by tigers in five years.

The savannah grass (we called it elephant grass) was up to 12 feet high and was tunneled with networks of muddy human and wild boar trails. The human trail tunnels were taller than the boar trails but not much wider. The tigers' stripes, it was obvious, would blend right in to the upright pattern of the grass.

George had an old 30.06 World War II rifle. *A tiger could make lunch of us before the safety could be released!* I thought to myself.

The villagers knew Rev. Loc and were happy to see him and, therefore, us. They were happy to see the gun as well. Wild buffalo were eating their rice crops and they wanted us to go out at night and shoot them.

George declined to go but told me I could go if I wished. Not having a good spotlight, I decided not to go either. The wisdom of that was later evident when I heard that in order to kill a buffalo one has to aim for the eyes so that the bullet will enter the brain through the eye opening. With skulls too thick for a bullet to penetrate, a charging buffalo would not be a pleasant sight.

Sitting around the fire box of our host's house, my eyes burned like coals with the smoke. I looked forward to sleep when I could close them, but closing them, I found out, only intensified the pain.

As I lay in the dark on the slats of the bamboo floor the strange new sounds of the village penetrated the walls—babies crying, men talking quietly, dogs nipping at each other, people urinating through the floors.

The village noises were finally drowned out as the wind howled and rustled the thatch roofs. All of a sudden I heard a noise. I knew it was a barking deer. An identical bark answered immediately.

"Hey, George," I whispered, "what was that second bark?"

I wasn't prepared for the answer.

"Tigers fool the deer by mimickng their bark," he said simply.

There was so much to learn. I lay in the dark praying, thinking, excited, enjoying every new experience—and hoping the tiger was more interested in the deer than in me.

✦   ✦   ✦

The trail passed through high valleys of towering grass and jungle. Short little Achu (Ah-CHEW), our guide for the trek, was clad only in Michelin tire-tread sandals and a loin cloth. He led the way. Pastor Loc trailed him wearing a pale blue fedora, white dress shirt, trousers and steel-belted radial sandals. He sang hymns in Vietnamese.

Heavyset George in khaki, pouring sweat and swatting huge deer flies, was third. He had a special chuckle, and he and Rev. Loc chatted and laughed a lot.

I was somewhat disadvantaged, not knowing the language. I brought up the tiger-bait position in the rear, wearing the latest American clothes, fresh from our missionary barrel. A comical sight to be sure!

Insects screamed a constant C note all around us. The sound at times was deafening. Myna birds alerted everything within hearing distance: "Humans are coming! Humans are coming!"

Our arrival in each village was always an event. Ordinarily the villagers dressed in tribal attire, but now they greeted us in shirts and trousers and toting Pan Am carry-on bags!

The villagers were so paranoid about tigers that in one instance just a pig's squeal started everyone beating on pots and pans, yelling, screaming, hoping that if a tiger had attacked the pig, their noise would frighten off the marauding animal. As it happened, just a couple of pigs were fighting and it was not a tiger at all.

A family invited us to have lunch. I can still see the young 18- or 19-year-old son—handsome, lithe, strong, clad only in a loin cloth—chasing our would-be meal through the village. That chicken, dressed and cooked together with rice, became a chopstick challenge for me. As I struggled to make them work, I noticed that the other guests who had gathered in the house were pointing at me and commenting among themselves.

"What's the matter?" I asked. "Why are they talking about me?"

"Oh," one of our companions answered, "they're afraid you aren't going to get enough to eat!"

As I struggled with those chopsticks, I, too, had the same fear!

The trip concluded with a typhoon, further adding to my store of memories. It came ashore just south of our location. All night the rain fell, driven by howling, gale force winds. The next morning, with the rain still pouring down, we set out to hike back to the vehicle.

On the precipitous descent, where the Bru had notched steps into the trail, a herd of elephants had preceded us. Their feet had torn off all the notches, creating in the process an almost vertical mudslide. All the way down that mountain we slid, bump, bump, bumping, first one of us in the lead, then the other.

Finally, after slogging through our fill of mud and blinding rain, weighed down with 50-pound backpacks and drenched to the skin, we reached the Jeep and piled in under the rag top.

George revved up the motor and soon we were on our way back to Danang, driving through 75-mile-per-hour winds and a flooded roadway. (Did I mention changing a flat tire in the storm, or that my nice new dacron raincoat—also fresh from the missionary barrel—stopped no rain at 75 miles an hour?)

The wind was still blowing when we reached Danang after dark. Hot, humid and dripping wet, I passed by EG with a quick hello kiss and headed straight for my razor. The trip was my first experience of not shaving my beard. It was the best shave of my life. EG, the soft bed and the wind soothed me to sweet slumber. It was good to be home.

That was only the first of several trips I would take with George through those northern provinces, learning to cohabit with huge deer flies, leeches and bedbugs. But it was good training— eating anything, sleeping anywhere, fearing nothing but God and loving everyone.

✦ ✦ ✦

It was fun living in Danang with the other missionaries. The competition of so many language-learners goaded us on to persist until we could speak fluently. And, like all rookie missionaries, we made our share of linguistic errors. A letter I wrote in 1958 reports the following:

> Today I got in a jam out in front of the house. I was taking pictures of things going up and down the street when I began to get a crowd around me. It got bigger and bigger as I used some of my Vietnamese. They

asked me how old I was and if I was married and I told them. Then they asked if I had a family.

I didn't know how to say "soon" or "in November" so I called Fleming (he knows more than I do). He told them. Then they asked him about his family. He doesn't have children so they offered to give him a child about 12 years old. He said *"khong"* (KHAWM) (no). Then they asked him if he wanted a Vietnamese wife, or another wife, so he could have a family. He didn't quite understand and answered "sure." When he realized what they had asked, he said *"khong* (no)" again. The joke was really on him. We tease him about taking applications for another wife.

In November EG and I traveled the 50 miles from Danang to Hue (WHAY), Vietnam's former imperial city. There, on November 14, at a little storefront clinic run by an American-trained Vietnamese doctor, we welcomed John Nathan, our firstborn. Although we had a small bassinet with a mosquito net for him, we finally brought him under our net because of the huge rats and cockroaches that were also spending the night at the clinic.

Few of us had vehicles, so we bought bicycles and rode all over the city. I remember carrying Nathan in my arm like a football as I pedaled to the Danang Vietnamese church.

In our free time, some of us former jocks got together at a Chinese high school to play basketball. We called ourselves "The Parsons." I can reach eight feet. The Chinese players jumped as high as they could and still only managed to hack at my arms. I always went home bruised from each game, and fouls were called only on me!

Those were idyllic months. We had no idea what the future held for us. It was just as well. Relative quiet had prevailed in South Vietnam since the French capitulation at Dien Bien Phu. There were reports of sporadic guerrilla activity in the outlying areas but the main population centers were secure. The South Vietnamese government, bolstered by American military advisers, appeared to be firmly in control.

But in January, 1959, not quite midway into our formal language study, North Vietnam's Central Executive Committee issued Resolution 15, changing its strategy toward South Vietnam from "political struggle" to "armed struggle."

None of us realized it then, but the Second Vietnam War had been declared.

4

Enough Adventure for a Lifetime

Late in 1959 we completed the prescribed Vietnamese language course. In some ways we were sorry to see it end. We had established solid friendships among our fellow missionaries and it was hard to tear ourselves away.

We would also miss the structured language-learning environment. Some of us were facing the need to learn an additional tribal language.

EG and I were assigned to Tra My (Traa ME), a settlement tucked among the precipitous mountains of north-central South Vietnam. I had been there once with George, but now I was on my way to get a place fixed up so EG and Nathan could join me.

I headed south from Danang. Thatched huts crowded to the edge of the unmarked pavement and children dashed across the road on whim. I crept through the crowd of people walking and selling on the roadway, forcing a tunnel. Glancing at the black exhaust of the Land Rover reflected in the rear view mirror, I watched the mass of humanity refill the road as I passed.

Both men and women carried heavy burdens slung from the ends of bamboo poles. Their large cone-shaped hats were held on their heads in the wind by opening their mouths wide against the chin strap.

About 50 miles farther down the road I turned due west and was soon surrounded by flat paddy land. Graves of ancestors rested beneath mounds of earth dotting the fields.

On the single-lane dirt road battered trucks, remade to resemble buses, groaned over the holes and bumps. People filled the wide-open interior of each truck/bus, and baskets of produce, chickens, tea, cloth, etc. balanced precariously on top. Men hanging by their hands from overhead rails stood on the running boards. Those with motion sickness lost their lunch down the sides.

The traffic was single file most of the way. I would get around one vehicle only to face the back of another. I would later realize just how enviously the passengers in those buses must have gazed at the empty seat and rear bed in my Rover.

As the flat lands gave way to small red hills and then steeper mountain grades, a steady stream of black-clothed Vietnamese manhandled bicycles loaded like pack mules with burlap bags of charcoal, tea, manioc or large bundles of firewood. Sticks tied to the handle bars extended them beyond the load for better control.

About half way to Tra My was the cinnamon town of Que-Son (Kuay SOHN)—"cinnamon mountain," which also had a large Tin Lanh church. I didn't know that cinnamon was the bark of a tree. Cinnamon trees grew around the houses like pecan trees in North Carolina.

Rumor had it that the Ngo family (the presidential family) fixed the cinnamon price very low. Being the only ones allowed to buy cinnamon, they then sold it high to world markets. Later, in protest, the people destroyed their trees rather than sell to the monopoly.

The road past Que-Son became steeper and turned to a dry stream bed. I gripped the wheel and geared in and out of the deep holes, the car plunging back and forth, wrenching me from one side to the other.

Another large Tin Lanh church about six kilometers from Tra My, my destination, was a welcome sight. The pastor and his wife offered me tea and bananas at a small table just inside the front door of their home. They were "too happy" to hear that we would be moving to Tra My.

I finally left the church and maneuvered the rest of the way into town. Tra My was pinched between two tree-clad hills. The first sight of civilization was a buffalo corral made of hewn logs. Many of the black long-horned beasts raised their heads just above the dung-colored wallow like alligators in a swamp. That was the town's first fragrance.

Many little thatch-roofed shelters and one tall shed housed the local market. Parrots, monkeys, venison, roots, fruits, snakes, birds, plants and garden produce were for sale. The tribesmen came to trade for salt that only the Vietnamese could supply.

I headed through the town and to the top of the

hill where our future home was perched. Black eyes
from private huts and yards lining the road focused
on the new car and the "western mister" driving it.
I stopped at the top of the hill and got out of the
car. The view west from our front yard was virgin
rainforest. A cleared bush-sprinkled slope dropped
gradually down to the banks of the clear, silt-free
Tranh River. Just beyond the boulder-strewn far
bank, trees taller than I had ever seen reached for
the sky. Vines, draped like sailors' ropes, spanned
the space from branch to earth.

I could live with this view forever, I thought to
myself. It attracted me. I wanted to look at it, to
feel it, to know it.

My reverie was broken as Mr. Sung and his "big
wife" (first wife) greeted me in the yard. He was so
excited to see me that he danced in his loose
pajama-like gray silk trousers and shirt.

He clasped his hands together beneath his chin
and bowed in greeting. I reached out and shook
both his hands with both my hands. He kept
saying, "Too happy, too happy." His one front
tooth did not make for clear speech. All his words
were caricatures of the Vietnamese I had studied.

I turned and greeted his wife deliberately so as to
include her. I clasped my hands together, bowed
and then also shook her two hands with my two
hands. The Sungs had been housesitting the
property for the Mission for several years.

We walked past their little rose garden and
climbed the two steps up to the cement floor of the
small thatched house. The house consisted of only
one large room, facing south. One glimpse told me

that the white lime-coated walls needed fresh cal-
cimine. The windows had bars and solid wooden
shutters, aged and unpainted. There was no ceiling.
The rafters and the thatch were in full view along
with whatever lived in the thatch.

The front door lead onto a narrow porch with an
overhanging roof. The only other door exited west
to a very smelly pigpen that had once served as a
kitchen. A thatched servant's quarters was at the
back of the house on the north side.

I drew a floor plan so I could explain things to
EG and began mentally making plans to fix the
place up. I would put a cement floor in the pigsty-
turned-kitchen. It would also need walls and windows. The walls of the house would be
recalcimined and I would put a ceiling in it.

The sunset was glorious. Something caused a very
purple cast to paint the sky. I had never before
seen a sky like that, nor would I ever see one again.
Perhaps it was God's special welcome to Tra My.

As darkness fell, a bright red smoky candle was lit
and placed between us on the small table. The
smoke was offensive and black as soot.

Mr. Sung served supper—broken red rice and a
vegetable named *shu* cooked with bits of chopped
chicken legs, bones and all. It was heavy on the
crushed black pepper and salty fish sauce. A metal
serving spoon served the food into ancient chipped
rice bowls which contrasted with the highly
polished ebony chop sticks. A porcelain tea pot
housed green jasmine tea for our mini-cups, also
old and chipped.

Dessert looked like a tray of chocolate-covered

Rice Krispies. It was Rice Krispies all right, but the dark stuff was duck blood. I did my best to not allow my face and mouth betray my stomach's revulsion. The apostle Paul had said, "I can do all things through Christ who strengthens me." So I ate two pieces of duck blood Rice Krispies, all the while thinking about the customary missionary table grace: "Lord, thank you for this food and protect us from it. Amen."

That prayer would express my sentiments many times in the future.

One "food" incident included Mrs. Marie Irwin, wife of E.F. Irwin Sr., the senior missionary at Danang. She had arrived there in 1911. When the Irwins retired in 1960 she was still in top physical form and could out-hike many of the younger women. Her three children—George, Franklin and Helen Mae—had all returned to Vietnam as missionaries and blessed the entire missionary force.

I once traveled with the Senior Irwins to a country church. During lunch I noticed that Mrs. Irwin ate everything on her plate except something that appeared to be a browned almond. (I was still quite food conscious!)

"Why don't you eat that?" I asked her.

"I don't like silkworm larva," she responded matter-of-factly.

I thought, *Well, if I'm gonna be here for 40 years, I am gonna at least try it.*

I snatched one of those things up in my chopsticks with a flourish and popped it into my mouth.

Have you ever stepped on a caterpillar? That is
how a silkworm larva bites!

It didn't taste bad but I didn't like the way it bit. I
joined forces with Mrs. Irwin. I didn't like 'em
either!

✦ ✦ ✦

After the meal came family devotions. Mr. Sung
got out some horn-rimmed glasses and read from
the book of Psalms. His poor vision and bare
literacy did not deter him, and he read very loudly
and very seriously. I enjoyed every minute of it. But
the best was yet to come.

Mr. Sung then got out his large worn Vietnamese
hymnbook and turned to "Rock of Ages." I brought
out my newly acquired hymnal. I have sung for
years, but when Mr. and Mrs. Sung began "Rock of
Ages"—and I tried to sing the melody along with the
Vietnamese tones—there was no sound I could
make that would harmonize. I tried bass. Nope!
Tenor? Nope. Alto? Nope. Melody? Not in this house!

The Sungs' faces glowed in the candlelight
against the inky black background. Even Mr.
Sung's one front tooth glowed. They were filled
with joy. It was all I could do to stifle my laughter. I
finally gave up trying to harmonize and together we
sang the song with joy: "Rock of ages cleft for me,
let me hide myself in Thee."

That night I heard the rats outside my mosquito
net.

✦ ✦ ✦

Back home in Danang I approached Loc, our cook. Loc was a thin young man with a shock of black hair and a captivating smile and spirit. He eagerly learned western cooking from EG. Coconut pie was his specialty.

Loc agreed to bring his wife and two children and move to Tra My with us. So we men went to get the accommodations ready for our families.

The actual move to Tra My was postponed so often that EG wrote in a prayer letter: "I refuse to write that we are leaving for Tra My this week since so many times it has proven otherwise. We went down the 27th but were unable to go all the way because a river was flooding over its bridge, making it impossible to cross." Another delay was caused by a miscarriage EG suffered.

We all finally arrived at Tra My. The cheap furniture we had piled into the truck was well "antiqued" in the jostling by the time it arrived. "Miz" Lois Alexander of McDonald, North Carolina had given us a country ham-grease-saturated "New Perfection" kerosene stove. But we had cleaned it up and crated it for the trip from America to Vietnam and now to Tra My.

Besides the stove, we had a kitchen table with four chairs and a couple of six-foot wide shelves that served either as a china closet or as a dresser, depending on the color of cloth one used to hang over the front and sides.

I sawed out the center of one of our four kitchen chairs to make a seat for our nighttime chamber pot. By day a piece of plywood covered the hole. That chair followed us everywhere in the highlands.

It was always a conversation piece.

It was great fun setting up our little "love nest" at the end of the road.

We moved into the house before the ceiling was completed. EG is the one who spotted the seven-foot serpent draped over the rafters overhead. "Charlie!" was a word I heard often as we settled into what would obviously be a temporary home. I finally put up a sailcloth ceiling to at least fend off the snake and lizard droppings.

When we were somewhat settled in, I began to lay plans for exploration into the surrounding areas. The road ended in our front yard so I already knew that any travel beyond this point would have to be on foot. I remembered the advice of a senior missionary: "Never ask a low official for permission to do anything. Always go to the chief. The lower official would love to exercise his small authority to say 'no.' "

So I went to the district chief and received permission to accompany "ruff puff" patrols (relatively untrained troops who patrolled the jungles looking for enemies of the government) on their excursions into the tribal villages.

The ruff puffs knew the trails and were armed. I had no firearm. I had to trust them. The only valuables I carried were a cheap watch and a used camera. Even the pots I used belonged to the cook who accompanied us. Besides those necessities I carried a notebook in which to write the results of my investigation into how many Jeh tribes lived in the area and how many different languages were spoken. This was part of a broad research study to determine the number of languages spoken in South Vietnam.

One day word came that a patrol would be going to Xa Bui (SAA Buoy). I drove to Danang to pick up missionary Dale Herendeen to accompany me on the trip. Dale was from California and played the piano like a professional. Herendeen, as we called him, was a great conversationalist. He was the senior missionary of the latest recruits and about 10 years older than I. It was exciting to be striking out on our own without George's advice and experience to rely on.

Dale, EG and I sat in the light of a beautiful glass kerosene lamp donated by one of the families of McDonald. It was a leftover from the pre-electric days in North Carolina. We read the Bible and prayed together before bedtime.

I found it hard to sleep as I lay beside EG in the dark. Now we were really on our own, away from the security of the missionary force in Danang. We discussed the fact that EG would be alone during my trips and agreed that having the Loc family there would help.

Sung and Mai (MY), our carrier and cook, showed up early in the morning. A hand-rolled banana-leaf cigarette was permanently fixed between Mai's teeth.

Iron-hard muscles hoisted the heavy baskets full of supplies onto the ends of the carrying pole. We walked over to the army camp. The troops were ready, dressed in green fatigues, "Ho Chi Minh sandals," bandanas, fatigue caps or big straw cone hats (called *nongs*) (NAWNGS). Each had a cloth tube of rice wrapped around his shoulders or in a small pack. Carbines or ancient French rifles were slung over their shoulders.

Many also carried a stick with a small bag tied to it. The bag contained a mixture of lime to kill the leeches that would be certain to attack their bare ankles. Most of the men were smoking hand-rolled cigarettes or chewing betel nut. They didn't talk much because their mouths were either full of betel or holding a cigarette.

We trekked north along the Tranh River, the trail quickly forcing us to walk single file. The cloudless sky gave way to the jungle canopy and soon we were climbing steep hills and crossing creeks, either by wading or swinging over vine and bamboo bridges tied to trees. I hated wet socks and shoes, so I removed both at each crossing. The Viets laughed.

After spending the first night in a mountain village, we separated ways from the soldiers and headed to Xa Bui guided by some Jeh tribesmen. The Jeh do not make gradual switchback trails. They simply aim for the ridge line at it's lowest point and carve out a stairstep to get there.

Xa Bui was 3,500 feet above sea level. Tra My was 350 feet above sea level. That meant a lot of climbing. One set of muscles got a workout as we headed 2,000 feet straight up the ridge. Another set got their exercise as we headed 1,000 feet down the far side and then up again to Xa Bui.

The village consisted of one single longhouse over a hundred meters (300 feet) long. There were apartments on either side of a long central hallway broken only by a large communal room in the middle of the building. It became our bedroom for the night.

Buffalo skulls with fresh rice stalks stuffed in their mouths adorned the walls. A large bundle of buffalo tails—a sacrifice to the spirits—also hung in the room. There were two fire boxes on the floor. The front of the house was on the ground, the back supported by 10-foot stilts.

Down the ridge was another large house but it was falling down, abandoned for some reason. Tall poles for sacrificing buffaloes to the spirits were just up the hill from the front door of the house.

Mai opened a tin of corned beef and cooked supper. Kids crowded around to watch. Curious adults ambled through and passed on.

Not being able to communicate with the Jeh spawned a passion in my heart to learn a tribal language quickly. I could not bear being unable to tell these people the message of Jesus that filled my heart.

After dark, by the firelight, Mr. Sung preached about God, the Lord of Heaven, to a packed house.

✦ ✦ ✦

Ted Cline was the next one to hike with me. I had noticed some place names on a map but when I inquired about them no Vietnamese would acknowledge their existence.

"No one knows the way," they responded. And, "You don't want to go there." I felt in my heart that the area had simply been left to the communists because of its isolation.

So Ted and I joined a ruff puff patrol across the river and into the deepest jungle I have ever seen. Leeches abounded.

My stomach was bothering me. I had made the mistake of drinking some water from a remote— and what I thought was a safe—creek on the last trip. However, amoeba live in tropical waters even where there are no people.

The amoeba began to plague me and for the first time I had to slip away from the group and pass bloody stools. Dysentery problems would plague me until I left Vietnam.

We hiked all day at a pretty slow pace, never seeing the sun through the dense jungle.

Toward evening the Vietnamese suddenly picked up the pace. I should have suspected something. We soon arrived at a small opening in the jungle, bordered by a rushing stream. Across the stream and 50 yards up there were a couple of thatched shelters. The soldiers beat us there and claimed the space.

The Jeh tribesmen with us fanned out to get supper—leaves and roots from the jungle, snails, clams and fish from the stream, plus, of course, the ever-present rice.

The only cleared spot for Ted and me turned out to be a dome-shaped boulder in the creek exactly at the point where the trail crossed the creek.

We rolled out our sleeping bags on the rock and pretended we were going to sleep there. As darkness fell the soldiers sang mournful songs about how hard life is: "Life has turned to hardship.

Death is even more difficult."

Gradually as the light of the fires faded, the sound of their voices faded, too.

The rock was not flat! We draped over it on our stomachs, laughing and joking about the unique accommodations. Eventually we fell asleep.

In the middle of the night the place lit up. Our eyes popped open to see that a full moon had risen above the jungle. As I lay there I thought, *You dummies! If a tiger uses this trail tonight, he will either step over you or eat you!*

In the morning it didn't take us long to roll up our beds, eat our corned beef and green beans and move out once again onto the trail.

Some hours later we exited into a clearing with a Jeh village. About 25 people lived there in just a few small houses. The nearest village, they said, was two more days' walk away. Within a radius of a two-day walk of Tra My, we had found only about 2,000 Jeh.

That night Mr. Sung preached again. And again I determined to learn a tribal language as quickly as possible so that I, too, could share the good news.

Morning brought another meal of the ill-tasting red broken rice. I caught Ted dumping his bowl out the window to the pigs down below.

"This stuff tastes like rubber bands," he commented.

Two Jeh agreed to lead us back to the river. There were no guns in our party this time, so we were startled when two close-cropped young Vietnamese with rifles came running past us. I suspected something was amiss. I had never seen Viets run anywhere.

When we arrived back at the creek where we had slept on the boulder, the thatched buildings had been torched and were still smoking. I have always assumed that the two we had seen were Viet Cong.

Back in civilization, I drove Ted back to Marjorie in Danang. Late that night I returned to EG. Nine months later, the Clines gave birth to Robin and the Longs gave birth to Edward within three hours of each other!

✦   ✦   ✦

It seemed that each day in Tra My brought new and exciting experiences. We used a bucket for bathing, a ritual which was carried on in the living room. A five-foot-tall Vietnamese carpenter measured my six-foot-four frame with his meter stick to custom-make the outhouse which was about 50 feet behind the main house.

The river served as the bathing and laundry place for the villagers. There were always people noisily working and playing there. One day I saw a man trailing a very large fish on a rope over his shoulder. He had caught it just below our house.

A few days later when a soldier invited me to go fishing with him I enthusiastically accepted. I soon learned that we would be fishing not with a hook and line but with hand grenades.

We walked about three miles along the river until we came to a hill. At the base of the hill the river flowed up against a huge flat, 100-foot long rock, forming a deep pool. The three little boys who had accompanied us were placed strategically on the rock to catch the stunned fish as they came to the surface of the water.

I had had a bad experience as a kid when a firecracker went off in my hand so I stayed well back while the soldier chucked the first grenade into the water. We saw no fish so he pulled the pin on number two and threw it. Little fish splashed all over. The boys plunged in, plucking them out of the water and throwing them up on the rock.

While the soldier filled his basket I walked out onto the rock and began to eye the stream. A fish tail as wide as my hand splashed 20 feet downstream. I yelled at the kids but they were occupied with all the little ones.

I wanted that fish! So I stripped off my clothes and dived in. The water was deep and moving fast. I managed to reach the fish and tried putting my thumb up in his gills. When I touched him he dashed away.

As both the fish and I continued downstream I finally managed to penetrate his right gill and get a good hold on him. With the fish secured, I made my way to shore. To my dismay I discovered that I was about a mile downstream from my clothes which were still out in the middle of the river on the rock.

Bare as Adam I gingerly made my way along the riverbank, toting a seventeen-kilo fish. In fishing English that is 37.4 pounds! *If the missionary prayer band at Toccoa Falls College could see me now!* I thought, grinning to myself. It was the largest catch of the day.

Meanwhile, back at home, my ever-faithful wife, sweetheart, alter ego, friend and mother of Nathan, lived in the thatched house at the end of the road getting her own introduction to tribal ways and customs.

One cool evening EG and I were strolling through the lanes of Tra My. Everyone was friendly, cordial—and curious about us. As we passed the house of a Vietnamese cinnamon trader an inebriated Jeh chief, whom I had met up in the mountains, saw me and came tottering over to the edge of the road to greet us. I turned to him, bowed low and shook his right hand (a carryover from French days).

The chief proceeded to greet me in even more French style—kissing me on each cheek. That would have been all right except that the Jeh had the custom of kissing one cheek then spitting red betel nut juice over the shoulder of the "kissee" before turning to the other cheek and doing the same.

Unfortunately, the chief failed to notice EG standing directly behind me in his line of fire.

As we walked away, EG muttered, "Couldn't he see me?"

"Sorry about that, honey," I responded sheepishly. "I forgot to tell you about that old Jeh custom!"

✦ ✦ ✦

The Vietnamese pastor of a nearby Tin Lanh church asked me to join him in evangelizing a Viet-

namese village close to where we lived. Our introduction to the village came through a friendly family who invited us for dinner.

Their home was elevated like ours. For fear of
snakes, scorpions and other harmful creatures, a
20- to 30-foot area around it had been cleared of
all vegetation. Close to the kitchen, however, there
were manioc plants, peppers, papayas, guavas,
bananas, tomatoes, pineapples and an assortment
of herbs and other edibles.

Nathan, of course, always attracted a curious
mob. The women in this village had not seen a
Caucasian child before. They chattered and
crowded close, wanting to hold him, pinch him and
check out his sex beneath his diaper.

Our host and hostess managed to push back the
crowd while we ate our dinner of steaming rice,
manioc, chicken (including heads and feet) sauteed
with local vegetables and, of course, *nuoc mam*. For
dessert there was black bean custard with coconut
milk topping. This became our most enjoyable
Vietnamese dessert. In fact, Vietnamese food was
usually very good.

The hanging pressure lantern under which
Grandma served us from china bowls cast shadows
on a red casket perched overhead in the rafters.
When I asked about it, Grandma said it was hers.
Should she die suddenly, she explained, there
would not be time to order one made. Her casket
was ready for use whenever she needed it.

After dinner, by lantern light, EG played her ac-
cordion and we sang for the hundreds who
gathered. The Vietnamese pastor told the story of

Jesus Christ from Genesis to Revelation. Time
meant nothing. This was a major event in the village. Some received Christ as their Savior.

The next night, in a village on the ridge just above
where we were meeting, the first communist in-
filtrator that I had heard of was killed in a gun battle. The local district chief buried his body in an
open pasture within sight of our home.

✦ ✦ ✦

Returning from one of my trips to the jungle, I
found the green area around the district compound
covered with Jeh refugees. They had carried what
they could in baskets on their backs. The elderly
and babies were there, too. Even their dogs were
with them.

I walked among them with the district chief.

"The communists killed our leaders," they said.
"They burned our village. Our people are scattered.
They are not all here and we don't know where they
went. We ran into the jungle and regrouped there.
We walked three days to get here."

All the district chief could say was, "We just don't
have the things we need to fight the communists
here. I wish they would give us more men and
weapons."

I wrote in my diary:

Late this evening the remaining refugees
came down and are the most pitiful yet.
One woman still had blood on the back of
her legs from giving birth. There were three

or four old women, very exhausted, and three or four women with new babies. All were very tired. We cooked wild boar rice gruel (*chao*) for them and fed all the women.

I cannot describe the pity, compassion, sickness, anger and wrath that I felt for them all at once over the cause of their distress—communism and its dark, devil-bound teachings and deceit. May God let me live to see it—whether in body or in spirit—perish from the earth and the glory of God Himself shine in the place of its darkness.

Jeh stragglers kept coming for days. We had a daily lineup at our house looking for medicines.

By the time we had been at Tra My six months it was evident from our research that most of the Jeh tribespeople we wanted to reach were on the other side of the mountain. We sought permission from the authorities to move to the region, but because of the intermesh of politics and religion in the Diem government we were not granted permission.

✦ ✦ ✦

It was conference time. I was just 24 years old. I felt that I had to report that the Jeh would be better reached from the west. And, as if to bolster our report, while we were away, one of the ruff puff patrols was ambushed. Six were killed and 16 wounded.

The conference decided to appoint us to Khe

Sanh (Kay SHUN) and the Bru people on the northwestern border of South Vietnam, about six miles from Laos and six miles from North Vietnam.

As it turned out, our departure from Tra My was none too soon. We left in May and in September some Viet Cong, looking for "the Americans," shot up and burned our Tra My home.

I remember Tra My as the most beautiful place we ever lived.

5

The Jarai

If our stay in Tra My was short, our stay in Khe Sanh was, as the GIs would later say, a "short-short."

Khe Sanh was a Vietnamese village central to the Bru tribe and just a few kilometers south of the demilitarized zone (DMZ). EG once again waited in Danang while I set up housekeeping.

July 5, 1960 she wrote: "This week Charlie is supposed to be getting our house set in order so that he can take us up when he comes back. We still don't have permanent permission to live there but believe it will come in good time."

We did move there. Our bedroom faced north toward communist Vietnam and Red China. As we slept each night our feet pointed in that same direction. I did not like the feeling!

U.S. Aid had purchased two-and-one-half-ton Toyota military trucks for the Vietnamese army. Three similar trucks without military markings and painted a different shade of green made regular runs along Route 9 into Laos. I asked one of the tailgate keepers what they were doing. He said that the president's family was trading in Laotian coffee while keeping prices fixed on Vietnamese coffee. It was like the cinnamon racket at Tra My!

We had been in Khe Sanh only two weeks when permission to live there was denied. We were told that they could not guarantee our safety and they asked that we move somewhere else.

At the time no Caucasian missionaries were ministering among the large Jarai (Jaa RAI) population in and around Pleiku (Play KOO), although there had been Alliance work in the area since 1948. Of all the Montagnards (mountain tribes) inhabiting the highlands of South Vietnam, the Jarai were the most numerous. The conference assigned EG and me to the Jarai tribe. Our base of operations: Pleiku.

Pack up and move! Pack up and move! We were learning early that missionaries are mobile. A rare few spend most of their working years in a single location. All others had better be prepared for periodic, even frequent, dislocations.

We set out in our trusty Land Rover—EG and I, with Nathan swinging a long-handled wooden spoon at anything in reach—together with what baggage we could shove in. A stake-bodied truck followed, once again battering our cheap furniture over the bumpy roads south to the red-dirt city of Pleiku.

It was July, 1960.

We had been in Pleiku less than 48 hours when the Jarai Christians invited us to a dinner in our honor at the home of the pastor. They had prepared a big feast to welcome us.

We enjoyed the food and had a great time of fellowship with the believers. Later, as EG and I were sitting in our living room, the pastor and a deacon arrived.

"Are you sick yet?" they asked with obvious concern.

The question seemed strangely out of context.

"What do you mean, 'Are you sick yet?' " I wanted to know.

"Well, everybody who ate with us has become ill. They are all vomiting. We think it was some bad cooking oil that one of the men got from the airfield."

We were glad to reassure the callers that we felt fine.

They were hardly away from the house when EG jumped up and rushed to the bathroom.

I'm not going to be psyched by all this, I decided. *I don't feel sick and I'm not going to get sick!*

I continued to read my book. But in a few minutes my stomach did three spins and I followed EG to the bathroom.

It was a great welcome to Pleiku!

Despite the unfortunate beginning, EG and I felt at peace about Pleiku. After two false starts we were glad to be in a place that gave us some promise of permanence. And we were thankful to be in a comparatively peaceful part of the highlands.

Our first order of business would be to learn the Jarai language. We were still becoming proficient in Vietnamese but few of the Jarai, we discovered, spoke Vietnamese. It was like hitting a linguistic brick wall. We would have to begin from point zero all over again.

EG and I soon made a second discovery: independent language study in the highlands was very different from the supervised tutorial situation we had known at Danang. Our language informants came from wherever we could recruit them, but I was determined to learn Jarai in the shortest possible time. That meant eight to ten hours of language study six days a week. One month of that pace and the first informant tired out and went back home to his village.

His replacements took on the same habits— working for a month or so then going back to their village. Some would stay there and rest a while and then be ready for another stint. We seemed to be constantly looking for language informants.

✦ ✦ ✦

Pleiku was the heart of Jarai country (*Plei* is the Jarai word for "village" and *Ku* means "tail"; thus, "the village of the tail"). The French built Pleiku to be an administrative center for the Jarai, perching it atop a 2400-foot-high plateau.

Until the French left in 1954, Vietnamese were not allowed in Pleiku unless they were employed by the French. After the defeat of the French at Dien Bien Phu and their departure from Southeast Asia, the complexion of Pleiku changed radically. The town became a Vietnamese provincial capital.

By the time we arrived, the population was about 5,000. Besides the Jarai, most of the residents were Vietnamese government and military people and their dependents, plus a few Chinese merchants.

The Vietnamese considered Pleiku their country's political Siberia for government workers. They were used to the sultry coastal plain or the equally hot Mekong delta. In addition to the "frigid" climate and epidemic levels of malaria that plagued the town, the Vietnamese also feared the primitive, animistic tribespeople who lived throughout the area.

Moreover, few of Pleiku's streets were paved. In the rainy season as much as 184 inches of rain fell in the space of six months. During that time Pleiku became a mud hole. In the dry season it was a dust bowl—a red dust bowl.

We, however, welcomed the stimulating mountain climate. The large villages that radiated out from the city in all directions afforded abundant opportunity for evangelism. We were sure God did not discriminate between the tribal people of the mountains and the more dominant Vietnamese. He loved them all equally. He desired all of them to repent and believe the good news of a Savior.

So Pleiku became the focal point for a renewed evangelistic work among the extensive Jarai population and the Vietnamese newcomers. With four-wheel-drive vehicles we had year-round access to even the remotest villages. And the Church of Jesus Christ began to take root, both in Pleiku and its environs.

✦ ✦ ✦

It was 1960. Back in "the world"—as the American GIs would later refer to the United

States—President Dwight D. Eisenhower, in a speech at Gettysburg College, had pledged the United States to maintain South Vietnam as a separate state free from North Vietnamese domination. Some 800 American military advisors were already in South Vietnam helping to train an armed force of 243,000.

Meanwhile, North Vietnam had imposed military conscription and Ho Chi Minh had begun infiltrating his cadres across the borders into the South.

That November, John F. Kennedy was elected president. Six weeks later, on December 20, North Vietnam announced the formation of the National Liberation Front.

Without a doubt, the 34-year struggle for the domination of South Vietnam was heating up.

6

The Seed
of the Church

Not all our Jarai language study took place within the confines of our home. EG, of course, was restricted by the care of Nathan and his new little brother, Robert Edward—Eddie. He was born December 19, 1960 at Banmethuot (Baan-me-TOO-it), a provincial center about 100 miles south of Pleiku. The Alliance operated a large hospital there, primarily for the care of leprosy patients. On the same trip I took the opportunity to have my tonsils removed.

I remember it well. I sat on a table in the operating room so that my head was about even with those of Dr. Ardel Vietti and Dr. Dick, a Mennonite surgeon who happened to be at the hospital at the time.

As I looked out the window that was directly behind them, I felt a needle go into each side of my throat. Once the novocaine had taken effect, Dr. Dick ran a needle with a suture through the tonsil to keep control of it as he looped a wire snare of a pistol grip device over it. He pulled the trigger. The loop sliced through, removing the tonsil and sealing the wound. I felt nothing.

Unfortunately my luck was not to hold. Dr. Dick began the same procedure on the left tonsil but the snare wouldn't work. Time ticked on as the doctors tried to fix it.

"I think the anesthesia is wearing off," I said after what seemed like an hour.

Dr. Dick picked up a scalpel and, with a sawing motion, began to extricate the tonsil. Each "in" stroke caused a gag reflex that sprayed blood over the doctors' white gowns. Before the operation was finally completed, we were all a bloody mess.

✦ ✦ ✦

Language learning is closely linked with knowledge of the customs and culture of the people. I decided that the best way to get the story of the people was to travel with the Jarai and Vietnamese pastors as they made their visits to outlying villages.

At first they did all the preaching. I was simply a means of transportation to get them to their preaching points. But the villagers enjoyed my sometimes feeble attempts to communicate and were always ready to speak into my recorder and tell their stories. This was how I learned the story of Ga Hao (Ga HOW).

Ga Hao was the leader of the area's Jarai Christians and the pastor of the mother church in Pleiku. His father had once joined in the fearful worship of the spirit gods that the Jarai believed inhabited everything from the forest tigers and deer and planted rice fields to the trees and rocks and communal longhouses in which the people lived.

Everything that the Jarai did was oriented to their fear of these spirits and their need to placate them. If a new longhouse was built it could not be occupied until all who worked on it sat down to drink the ceremonial rice wine that would appease the spirits.

Sickness also demanded a sacrifice. The sacrifice might be something as small as an egg if the illness was not severe; could be as large as a buffalo if the illness was life-threatening.

Ga Hao's father was the first in his family to let Jesus Christ break the binding shackles of the spirits. Someone from Banmethuot had witnessed in Ga Hao's village and his father and several other villagers had believed.

A small Tin Lanh church was built and it was there Ga Hao and his brother and sister came to know the Lord.

In the course of time Ga Hao attended the Bible school in Banmethuot and was assigned to be the pastor of the Pleiku Tin Lanh Church. He was a humble, unassuming man. Being pastor of the central church in Pleiku did not inflate his ego.

In many ways Ga Hao was not your typical pastor. He often appeared sloppy, with his shirttail untucked and the tongues of his boots hanging out. When the weather was cold he wore an old red V-neck cardigan that EG had given him—a one-of-a-kind in Pleiku.

Ga Hao could be eccentric, too.

"Oi Dlong (Grandfather Long)," he announced one day, "I'm seeing double."

"What's wrong?" I asked.

He told me he'd drunk a cup of gasoline to kill intestinal worms.

"Gasoline?" I exclaimed. "That stuff will make you blind."

"But somebody told me it would kill worms," was his response.

"You forgot the rest of the treatment," I jested. "You're supposed to light a match after you've drunk the gasoline!"

For all his eccentric ways, Ga Hao was a man of God. I was present when he prayed for a man in a distant village. The man was insane. He had been carrying a lighted torch around the village, threatening to burn it down. In self defense, the villagers had put him in stocks.

At the time I did not know the Jarai language. I could not understand the man's problem or the prayer Ga Hao was offering for his deliverance.

"Lord," I prayed simply as Pastor Ga Hao prayed, "whatever Ga Hao is asking for, please do it!"

Some months later we were back in the village.

"What happened to the man who was in stocks?" I asked.

"Oh," came the reply, "he's out in the field working. He hasn't been sick even one day since you prayed for him."

It was February, 1961. EG and I had been in Pleiku just six months when Ga Hao received a note from his extended family asking him to come home. They said they needed to talk with him.

In those days any communication from home was disconcerting. I remember the worried look on his face as he waved goodbye.

EG wrote home in February of 1961:

In the past two weeks, if experience adds to maturity, we've aged a few years. Two weeks ago last night while our pastor here was visiting in his home village, the Communists came in and took him away.

Charlie and the pastor's brother, Brao, went back this week again to see if there was any definite news about him but there was nothing certain. However, the village folk there say that he is surely dead.

Our hearts want to refuse this thought and continue to hope that he will still return. But as days pass into weeks and the knowledge of what has happened to others who have fallen into the communists' evil clutches surfaces, our hope begins to fade. Surely this is Satan at one of his most evil moments.

Ga Hao was a young man—about 35— and has four young children, the oldest about 8, and his wife is expecting another child any day now. Pray for her. If she has to return to her village she will be the only Christian there.

By the way, Brao's life is threatened too, to the extent that the village wouldn't let him spend the night lest he be taken in like manner as his brother. Brao is also one of our pastors. Should Ga Hao not return, that

leaves us with four national pastors in a tribe
of 200,000!

As you might expect, Ga Hao was our best man,
spiritually mature and a real witness of God's
saving grace. Through it all we know that His way
is best and we are not to question His working, but
it shall be a glorious day when He returns to bring
justice and then we'll know all the whys!"

What Ga Hao did not know when he got the letter was that some of his fellow Jarai tribespeople,
resentful that he was urging this people to turn
from the spirits and follow Jesus Christ, were seeking revenge. So they started a rumor that the
Americans were about to give Ga Hao a Jeep because he was working for the CIA.

It was all the communists needed.

Back in his home village Ga Hao sought out the
longhouse where the local Jarai pastor lived. And
that is where the Vietnamese communists found
him after dark that night.

First they tied his arms and hands behind his back.
Then they forcibly dragged him from the longhouse.

"It doesn't make any difference what you do to
me," Ga Hao gasped between stabs of pain. "The
Jarai are going to hear about Jesus Christ. They are
going to follow Him!"

Those were the last words any of the villagers
heard Ga Hao utter. Little did they or we realize at
the time how prophetic those words were. They
foretold the third love story that forms a part of
this book: God's love for the mountain people of
Vietnam.

It is a story cosmic in scope, a story that has been unfolding for more than 60 years as Jarai and other tribespeople have turned and continue to turn to the Lord in increasing numbers.

It is a story unimagined by me in that long-ago August, 1953 when I gave my heart and life to Jesus Christ. His love for those tribespeople would someday inspire the deepest awe I have ever felt.

The communists simply took Ga Hao away.

Rumors later reported that his captors, having tied his arms and hands together behind his back, threw the other end of the rope over the limb of a tree. When his body was completely suspended in the air, they took a Jarai sword and began chopping.

Feet.

Ankles.

Calves.

Thighs.

Piece by piece.

When they finished, Ga Hao was dead.

7

Love with Two Hands

When I received the word about Ga Hao I was devastated and angry. Who were these communists, anyway, who brutally tortured to death an innocent man of God wholly devoted to bettering the lives of his own people? And what would the church in Pleiku do now that it had no pastor? Was this to be the fate of all the evangelical Christians in South Vietnam?

And what about EG and me? If they did this to a Christian pastor, would Christian missionaries be next? Suddenly death and sacrifice became very real issues for me and I decided to make some basic changes in our lives.

After Ga Hao's murder EG no longer traveled with me but stayed at home to be a mother to the children in the event I should be gunned down along the roads or in the villages.

EG wrote my folks:

> Just this week the Reds have begun to "activate" again. It was really quiet for a couple

of months. At Banmethuout they ambushed a group of government officials and killed seven. One was the Jarai representative to the national assembly. Only a year ago he had come to know the Lord and was truly a faithful witness even in his high official position. It would seem that Satan would try to completely destroy the church among the Jarai by removing all who are leaders. But God knows how and why He desires to allow these men to be taken from us, and in His great plan His perfect will is being done.

The threat of danger made me both cautious and bold. I was cautious about being in public view but I was more bold than ever to tell others about Jesus and eternal life. We had all been branded by Ga Hao's murder. I felt a need to make his death worthwhile. I gritted my teeth and prepared to pay the price.

As I traveled the roads—1,500 kilometers a month—I talked to myself: *Let God alone be your fear, Charlie! Let God alone be your fear, Charlie.* And a phrase from Shakespeare kept circulating in my mind: *Screw your courage to the sticking place.*

With only six months of Jarai language study behind me I preached in the Pleiku church practically every Sunday until a new pastor could be found. There simply was no one else to do it.

Beside our language study and my preaching, we were faced with another challenge. One area pastor in particular had been pleading with us to help the many Jarai who had leprosy. Until I arrived in

Pleiku, leprosy was a disease I had never seen and knew nothing about. But here among the Jarai I could not avoid the terrible condition of many of its victims. Yet in all of the province there was no place where they could receive care.

When Eddie was delivered at the leprosarium/ hospital near Banmethuot we had the opportunity to learn firsthand about the work the hospital was doing.

The Leprosarium had been founded by Gordon H. Smith, the Alliance pioneer among the mountain tribespeople of Vietnam. It was the first such facility operated by The Christian and Missionary Alliance in South Vietnam and over the years it became a showpiece for leprosy ministry.

Convinced at last that we needed to address the leprosy problem in and around Pleiku, I contacted Banmethuot.

"Can you send someone to care for the leprosy patients up here?" we begged.

The people at Banmethuout were sympathetic but they had no worker to spare. They did, however, have a proposal.

"We can't provide a worker," they replied, "but we're willing to teach you how to care for them."

So we began to hold monthly leprosy clinics in Pleiku led by a missionary nurse from Banmethuot. The first clinics were conducted on the tailgate of my Land Rover. But as word spread and the number of patients increased we gradually erected a series of little thatch-roofed buildings in outlying areas. The patients themselves built the simple structures along roadsides isolated from any village.

Every 28 days we made the rounds of those

clinics to treat the patients that gathered there. We checked each one, taking blood serum samples (known as BIs [bacillus index]) to be checked for Microbacteria Leprae by lab technicians and dispensing the monthly supply of medicine. If the disease was advanced, we would transport the patient the 100-plus miles over poor and frequently dangerous roads to the Banmethuot Leprosarium for inpatient care.

The Plei Thoh (Play TUH) clinic drew the most critical patients out of the woods. There was a reason why the leprosy in this area seemed more serious.

The Jarai believed that Lake Bien Ho, north of Pleiku, was a volcanic crater that had exploded years earlier. A 35-kilometer-wide plateaued area near the lake is without large trees to this day and there are areas where pumice is scattered over the ground. Many of the Plei Thoh area patients needed longterm care because of the abrasions the pumice caused to their feelingless feet.

It was my practice at Plei Thoh to hold a clinic all day then have the severely debilitated patients remain overnight. The following day I would drive back the 55 kilometers to pick them up and take them to the Leprosarium 155 kilometers away in Banmethuout.

"Spend the night here and I'll take you to the hospital tomorrow," I repeated one particular day. By nightfall I realized I had made 28 promises but my vehicle could hold 14 at the most. That meant two trips.

The next day I started early to Plei Thoh to collect the first load. With the vehicle packed to the roof we were under way. It was dry and dusty, a long, uneventful trip.

With the patients delivered, I picked up a loaf of French bread at a stand by the edge of the road and climbed back in the car. A few miles down the road I noticed that since my inbound trip the Viet Cong had stuck a stick in the roadway. A VC flag (half red, half blue, with a gold star in the center) and propaganda leaflets were placed in the split end of the stick. I slowed down but decided to go on without stopping.

Back at Plei Thoh I picked up the other 14 passengers and roared off to Banmethuot again. This time I stopped and picked up the flag and leaflets.

From kilometer 70 to kilometer 110 the road tunneled through the jungle near the place where Ga Hao was taken. After kilometer 110 the road switched back and forth up a sandy mountain of bamboo-laden terrain. Then came open grassland where one could see for miles. Then the rubber plantations with long, even rows of the great shade trees tapped with collecting cups adorned the landscape. At the end of the road—Banmethuot.

The trip was long and lonely. No refreshments. No facilities. Just a dry, dusty road and a cobra longer than my car. That day I drove about 515 kilometers and increased the patient load at Banmethuot by 28 people.

I arrived after dark at the Ziemers, tired, dirty, hungry, thirsty. When I was finally able to read the propaganda, it said, "Soldiers, do not make war on us. We are your brothers trying to free you from the imperialists who would destroy you!"

✦ ✦ ✦

Although leprosy is not highly contagious, it *is* contagious, and segregating those with the disease was a step toward controlling its spread as well as preserving them from violence from "well" people.

Some of those little isolated clinics became the nuclei of segregated villages where the leprous could live in community. There might be as many as 15 to 20 houses, together with the clinic building and a chapel. In all our humanitarian work one hand was for medical aid and the other for the gospel of Christ. We tried never to forget our primary reason for being in Vietnam.

With the ministry load increasing almost on a daily basis, we soon found it necessary to add a Christian Jarai tribesman, Mip (MEEP) by name, to our staff.

There was a large crowd waiting for us as we arrived at a village clinic called My-Thach (My THAT). They were seated on the ground, fanned out in the unmerciful sun on one side of the 10- by 10-foot shelter. There was no shade.

Mip taught them "Jesus Loves Me" and told them how this Jesus had made a way to heaven for everyone. He closed with "Only Trust Him" and we began the examinations.

Mid-day was blistering hot. The odor was nauseating, worse than usual.

"Mip, go see if you can find that really bad ulcer," I finally said, "and we can take care of it."

Mip checked out the crowd but could find no bad ulcer, at least not bad enough to cause the terrible smell. But he did find the source of the problem. A dog had hauled a rotten buffalo bone into the shelter!

Sometime in the afternoon I began to come to the end of my strength. I was hot, thirsty, hungry. The smells, the ulcers, the filth were causing me to feel sorry for myself. *I am only 25,* I muttered to myself. *I could be making it big in the USA.* My mind was thousands of miles away from the ulcerated foot that I was bandaging with bedsheet bandages rolled by the Alliance Women.

As I finished tying the knot, a voice inside me said, *Those are My hands.*

Tears welled up in my eyes as I recognized the Shepherd's voice.

They are Yours as long as You want them, I responded. The patient probably never understood why the missionary was crying.

Ultimately EG, Mip and I were treating 650 to 700 leprosy sufferers in the Pleiku area. Such an extensive operation demanded something more than the tailgate of a Land Rover and a corner of a house for supplies. So the Leprosarium erected a sizable metal building on the Mission property in Pleiku to serve as office and warehouse for the leprosy ministry.

✦ ✦ ✦

On November 13, 1961, EG wrote the first of several letters she would write home over the next three weeks.

We've celebrated Thanksgiving today, very aware that all we have comes from Him. We celebrated true Southern style—almost. The only thing lacking was the visit of the relatives! For dinner we had roast peacock (a 10-pound one Charlie killed last Thursday), mashed potatoes, dressing, candied yams, jello salad, a cranberry sauce, pickles, beans, hot rolls and pumpkin pie and coffee. How does that sound? Not much like the mission field, does it?

We got your letter today with the news of the evacuation of Pleiku. Boy, was that news to us! No such thing has happened. In fact, it is the lack of activity by the VC that is so bewildering now. Since October things have been quieter than they have been in over a year. We wonder if and when something will happen.

The second letter went to her mother just one week later.

There are 23 shopping days left—funny how things so minor as an ad in a paper are remembered, isn't it? Another year is almost gone. The Lord has been good, proving Himself to be sufficient for all things. The coming year I trust we shall learn to trust Him more fully for all things, be they great or small. To Him there is no difference, He is anxious to hear and answer our every call.

And on December 9:

> From now until Christmas we will really
> be busy. The leprosy clinics are next week.
> The following week I have to make costumes
> for our Christmas program. I want to have a
> ladies' meeting next week too, and then on
> the 23rd we'll be going to the villages for
> services and baptisms.
>
> Today I had my first ladies' meeting for
> the Jarai women. There were six here and
> they said they'd like to make it a regular
> thing. The Jarai have a matriarchal system
> and it would seem that if we could really
> reach the women there might be better
> response. The men seem to believe more
> easily than the women but more families
> might come if the mother believed.

EG's strategy for reaching the women worked,
and the ladies' groups continue to this day.

◆ ◆ ◆

In 1962 President John F. Kennedy ordered
Green Berets to Vietnam to begin training village
men as counter-insurgence defense groups
(CIDG). The mission of these American Special
Forces teams was to arm and train local villagers
not only to defend themselves from the Viet Cong
but to be points of strength to control the

countryside.

The smallest unit was an "A" Team. The smallest camps were "B" Camps, under the command of a "C" Camp. "B" Camps dotted our province.

One day a company of H-21 choppers—the banana-shaped, twin-rotor American helicopters— flew into Pleiku, descending on an old dirt runway, a remnant of the French war.

This unit of 200 American troops did not warrant a fulltime chaplain but, in response to their request, we hired some tribesmen to build a thatched bamboo chapel and began services every Sunday morning.

Many a Sunday I preached in Vietnamese, Jarai and English before lunch! I also held a memorial service for the first helicopter pilot, Chief Warrant Officer Charles Holloway, killed in action. The helicopter base was later named Camp Holloway in his memory. And before the American withdrawal there would be many such bases throughout South Vietnam, all named after the first American in the area to give his life in service to his country.

While on furlough in 1963-64 I wrote the following letter to Mrs. Holloway:

> Perhaps my name was mentioned to you in a letter by Major George Aldridge Jr. and I think that my wife wrote you a letter soon after your husband's death in Vietnam. We have been in the U.S. since July 1963. At the time of CWO Holloway's death I didn't think that anything that I might have to say

by way of letter could be of any consolation
to a wife and mother who had just lost her
husband in Vietnam. Just this weekend I
read an article in the October issue of *Red-
book* that caused me to change my mind and
write you.

My wife and I went to Vietnam in August
1958. Both of our children were born in
Vietnam. The first two years were wonderful
years. We were telling the good news of
God's love to receptive hearts. The Church
grew in Vietnam. In 1960, however, things
began to get grim. Terror stalked the land as
the communist guerrilla bands sent the
population near the edge of panic. It appeared that they would overrun the land and
that all missionaries would have to leave.

Our Vietnamese and tribal friends lived in
fear that the communists would take over
and persecute the Church. The year 1961
was especially bad. Two of my closest Jarai
friends were killed by the communists.
Many nights when I locked the doors of my
house I wondered what I would do if they
attacked my home and family. Vietnam was
losing the fight to preserve its liberty. That
liberty may not have been perfect, but we
missionaries were free to tell every man we
met of Christ, God's Son. Many were con-
verted in spite of great difficulties.

In the fall of '61 and spring of '62 the U.S.
began to give greater aid to Vietnam. Many
thousands of our men went to help a

country unable to help itself. The men asked me to be an auxiliary chaplain and I began to serve in March 1962 at the Pleiku detachment. I served the MAAG group, the signal corp, the Marines, the Air Force and the 81st helicopter transport company.

We made our house an open house to the men and did our best to make their time in Vietnam a little easier to bear. The helicopter pilots, with local help, built a small bamboo and thatch chapel. It was in that chapel that I held a memorial service for your husband.

The chapel was filled. Most every man that was off duty attended the service. When I held that service I did not believe that your husband had died in vain and neither did the men present that day. We all shared with you the agony of losing him. I distinctly remember tears in the eyes of his commander and yet you had to bear a very heavy burden all alone here at home.

Perhaps it would help you to know that we had 2,000 baptisms among the Vietnamese and the tribespeople during 1962. Had it not been for your husband and others, the missionaries would have had to flee Vietnam before 1962. I would like to think that Charles Holloway had some share in these 2,000 people who have found Christ as their Savior.

In spite of war and trouble, missionary work continues. It continues because some-

one cared enough for his country to give his
life. Mrs. Holloway, we do care about your
husband. We missionaries share with you
this heavy burden and we are humbly grateful for the many men who have served in
Vietnam. They have been used of God to
keep open doors that were shutting, doors
that would have closed out the preaching of
Christ Who gives everlasting life.

Missionaries, too, have suffered loss. Rev.
Archie Mitchell was captured in May 1962
by the communists. His wife and children
are still in Vietnam awaiting his release.

Many of the people of Vietnam also care,
Mrs. Holloway. A Vietnamese pastor was
stricken with grief when he heard of your
husband's death. That pastor has three
children that he hopes will never have to live
under communism. I am sorry now that you
couldn't have heard some of these things
back at the time of his death. I hope the
people of our nation will show a greater concern about Vietnam and the men who are
risking their lives there.

Some of us are very grateful and only wish
that it didn't have to be so. If I can ever be
of service to you or your family, please let
me know. I would count it an honor to serve
you who have paid so much and have been
rewarded so little.

"Come to me, all you who are weary and
burdened, and I will give you rest" (Matthew 11:28, KJV).

✦   ✦   ✦

War was about to become a way of life for most
missionaries in Vietnam, especially for those of us
serving in the highlands.

I often turned to Isaiah 8:13, the verse God had
given me before I left home: "Sanctify the LORD of
hosts himself; and let him be your fear, and let him
be your dread."

I was not eager to become a martyr in this nation
at war. I had a wife and two sons who, I liked to
think, still needed me. Naturally I shrank from
physical death.

But death, God had declared in His Word,
should not be my ultimate fear. To fall short of His
purposes, to miss His will for my life, was far worse
than physical death. My focus was to be on God
and His redemptive plan for the people of Vietnam.

I prayed that I would never fail Him.

8

Road Closed

It was late March, 1962. Mip, our Jarai helper in the leprosy work, and I were returning from a trip to the Banmethuot Leprosarium in the Land Rover.

Jarai farmers were burning the dried vegetation from their fields. Brown-white smoke and carbon ash mixed with the red dust to fill the atmosphere and give it a distinct, end-of-the-dry-season smell.

As Mip and I drove along, all the pressures of the past months seemed to drain away. I was relaxed. God was good. All was well. We surprised some flocks of wild jungle chickens. With my Remington automatic shotgun I bagged eight of them. Mip was all toothy smiles.

I felt great! I was young and vigorous. I could at last speak understandable Jarai. I had made new friends. I had a terrific wife and two healthy sons. Another baby was on the way. A man could not want for more.

I dropped Mip and six of the jungle chickens off and, at home at last, I presented EG with the other two chickens—complete with number six birdshot. EG is a great southern cook. I tease her that I fell in love when I tasted her mother's fried chicken! Suddenly that evening I was freezing cold. My teeth chattered. Then fever. *Malaria,* I thought. Well, I could fix that. I swallowed three chloroquine phosphate pills and went to bed.

But it was not malaria. Within a few days, the tell-tale jaundice of hepatitis was all too evident.

At first I did not know whether I would live or die. And I was too weak to care. Everything was an effort, even breathing. Any extra exertion could damage the liver. There were times when I felt as if I was out of my body, observing myself trying to go through the normal motions that were now nearly impossible.

Dr. Ardel Vietti made the trip from Banmethuot to check me over. But there is no magic pill for hepatitis. Time and plenty of bed rest are the prescribed cure.

"Eat lots of hard candy to put sugar in your system," Dr. Vietti advised.

Ama Tum (Aa-maa TOOM), the new Jarai pastor, and several deacons came to visit me. They formed a semi-circle around my bed and prayed for me. They could see how deathly sick I was. Yellow jaundice really shows on a white man! They were concerned. Would this missionary who had come to minister with them be taken from them?

As the weeks stretched on and those same men continued to pray, they saw me gradually improve. At last I was beyond the critical point. It seemed that I would probably stay with them after all. The illness had the effect of cementing us together. It earned me a secure place in their fellowship. They knew I was sincere.

Although I was in bed only six weeks, it would be eight months before I really felt well again.

Our annual Vietnam field conference was set for May. My American pastor, Rev. H.P. Williams, was the scheduled speaker. Hepatitis or not, I did not want to miss him, so I got out of bed and went to Dalat.

The conference was a refreshing time, strengthening both in body and spirit. After the conference, EG, with Nathan and Eddie and missionary Irene Fleming, left to go to Banmethuot to attend a seminar at the Leprosarium. Gail Fleming, Irene's husband, and I volunteered to give Pastor Williams a mini-tour of Vietnam and land him back in Saigon in time to catch his flight home. We would pick up our families at the Leprosarium in a few days.

By then the war was heating up. Ambushes on the highways were a frequent occurrence. But Pastor Williams wanted to see Vietnam and we were young enough and brash enough to show it to him.

On our way back down the coast from Danang we stopped at a grocery store to pick up some food. On a shelf we discovered a one-pound box of butter cookies imported from France. We included it with our purchases.

On down the road, as we entered a narrow valley, we were met by a line of army trucks parked along the shoulder. One of the drivers flagged us down.

"What's the matter?" Gail asked.

"The communists have set up a machine gun on top of the next hill. We're not going farther until we get reinforcements."

So there we were in the Land Rover—Gail Fleming at the wheel, H.P. Williams in the middle seat and I on the right—with the box of butter cookies on the dash in front of us.

While we were trying to decide what to do next, a freight truck pulled up behind us. We got out and explained the situation to the driver.

The trucker glanced up the mountain road.

"I'm going up," he said with determination. "I've got to get to Saigon." With that, he revved his motor, put the truck in low gear and started off around us. We decided to go too, following at a discreet distance to avoid getting involved in the event that he became the target of the machine gun.

As we bumped along behind the truck I thought of our missions course at Toccoa Falls College with Professor Gus Woerner. Every class began by singing all the verses of "From Greenland's Icy Mountains." As Gail moved through first, second, third and into fourth gear, I looked around at the scenery. *"Where every prospect pleases and only man is vile," really describes this,* I thought to myself. Off to the left a white sandy beach stretched along the aqua blue waters of the South China Sea. Dark areas in the water indicated coral reefs.

Several small boats lay upside down or on their sides beside grass shelters under the trees on the beach. At each end of the beach two heads of land rose several hundred feet above the water. Overhead, tall coconut trees protected thatched-roofed houses with lush green gardens. Bougainvillea splashed the area with its vibrant colors.

What a beautiful, private, beach-front village, I mused. *What a wonderful place to live! And what a horrible place to die or be shot and need medical help!*

Just beyond the village the road began its ascent over the southern head jutting out into the ocean. Gail had let the truck go on ahead out of sight. That was not difficult, for the road was a switchback which climbed to the top via a series of hairpin turns. Around any curve there could be the muzzle of the machine gun.

The Rover's sheet metal body was made of aluminum about one-sixteenth of an inch thick. *That would certainly not inhibit a 50-caliber slug,* I thought pessimistically.

Each open space after a curve without the gun was a relief. Gail was constantly shifting down, which made the engine rev louder and increased the whine of the transmission. If someone was there they couldn't miss us. *Lord, please take care of us,* I pleaded. *We are out of our depth!*

Gail geared down the pathetic little diesel still lower and I focused on the most distant visible point in order to quickly see whatever it was that we were about to see. Since the tallest hillside was on my side of the car, I stooped my head below the top of the window to watch the top of the ridge above. That would be a prime spot for the VC.

We were all silent. Gail was busy driving. I was busy staring. And HP never said a thing as each curve of the hill passed by, a clone of the last one. Around and around we went.

Is this a good day to die? Nope, I haven't met a good day to die yet! So far, so good. This ain't Mt. Everest.

We must be near the top.

At last Gail got out of second into third again. It felt good to go faster. We cleared the switchback curves and gained speed across the plateaued crest of the ridge.

No one had indicated exactly where the gun might be. Maybe the VC were set up in this impoverished village that we were approaching? The trucker was nowhere in sight.

Normally people would be standing around or bending over chopping wood, hoeing or doing the dozens of other chores typical of village life. But in this village the people were simply standing, looking—at what, we didn't know.

The reason soon became apparent. A truck, not the one preceding us, was sitting on the road completely blown apart. The crumpled remains of the cab was in one place. The body of the truck was in another.

"What happened to that truck?" we asked the bystanders.

"It ran into another truck," someone replied. We looked around. There was no evidence of a second truck.

"Yeah? Where is the other truck?" we probed further.

No one responded.

Recognizing that it was probably better to let the matter drop, we drove on down the road and out of the danger zone. When we finally arrived at our destination for the day I happened to look at the box of butter cookies on the dash board.

It was empty. In his nervousness, Pastor Williams

had eaten a whole pound of cookies!

✦ ✦ ✦

With Pastor Williams safely on the plane back to America, Gail and I headed the Land Rover northwest on the climb back up to Banmethuot and the Leprosarium. We were anxious to rejoin our families.

Having just been through enemy-infested territory, we were also concerned for our families. Were they safe? Had they experienced any problems while we were gone? Our concern, although we didn't know it then, however, should have been for ourselves. That very night we would come within a hair's breadth of death.

Vietnamese highways have no white or yellow lines. They are simply a narrow strip of blacktop defined on either side by grass growing right to the edge of the asphalt.

It was dark and raining heavily. In order to stay on the road I was driving on the left side where I could better see the line between the asphalt and the grass.

All of a sudden, a large orange road grader loomed before us in the headlights. But it was not moving—it was parked on the left side of the road. I hit the brakes and swerved to the right, missing the machine by inches. Had it been painted olive drab, as many were, we would not have lived to tell about it.

We thanked the Lord for his care over us and determinedly pressed on.

Much later that night, bone-weary, we rolled into Banmethuot and found our way to the row of French-style houses that dotted the Mission property. A light was still burning in one window. Our arrival was expected. Someone was waiting. It was a nice feeling.

The someone was Bob Ziemer.

"I hate to break this news to you when you're dead tired," he began as we entered the house, "but the Viet Cong have sealed off the Leprosarium road. We haven't been able to contact our people out there."

"Our people out there" included not only the resident staff at the Leprosarium but Gail's wife and my wife and children. And EG was five months pregnant.

It was the middle of the night. There was nothing we could do at that hour but pray. And I was too exhausted to do much of that.

I slept fitfully.

9

Long Day, Long Night

Despite our middle-of-the-night arrival in Banmethuot I was up early. The fate of my family at the Leprosarium 10 miles outside of town was uppermost in my mind. Gail must have been thinking similar thoughts. He, too, was up early.

It was Saturday, May 26, 1962.

As soon as we thought it wise to do so, we drove to where the road to the Leprosarium began. We wanted to have a look for ourselves. The first part of the road was little better than a wide trail. Across it the Viet Cong had felled giant, primeval trees—22 of them, we would later learn—totally blocking vehicular access to the road beyond and to our families.

A nearby sign also warned would-be travelers that the road was mined. "Danger—mines," said the sign written in charcoal on a large grass mat. "Who opens this road is an agent of Diem and will be beheaded."

I knew that the Viet Cong at that time typically

used undetonated 105- or 155-millimeter canon shells for their road mines, rigging them with lengths of fine wire. If a person stepped on or tripped over the wire, the tension pulled the firing pin on the shell, exploding it and inflicting injury or death on the unwary victim.

What bothered me was that our wives and my children were at the end of that road, accessible no other way!

✦ ✦ ✦

For the seven or eight North American missionaries normally staffing the Leprosarium there had not seemed a need for undue alarm up to that time. To be sure, communist troops had infiltrated the area, picking up sympathizers among the populace.

But the Leprosarium was a humanitarian operation established solely for the benefit of the people. The missionaries, although responsible to the central government, had no political agenda. They were prepared, in the name of Jesus Christ, to render aid to any victim of leprosy. And they did so.

But Gail and I had now been in South Vietnam several years. We had worked and traveled extensively throughout the central highlands. We knew the war was intensifying and we knew from experience some of the temper of the enemy. It had been hardly more than a year since they had brutally murdered Ga Hao, the Pleiku pastor. So when Gail and I found the road to the Leprosarium closed and allegedly mined, we had reason to fear the worst.

Banmethuot, under more peaceful circumstances, was a delightful tribal town high up on a jungle-clad tableland, surrounded by large rubber and coffee plantations developed years before by the French. The climate, especially for Western missionaries assigned to the hot, humid coastal plains, was wonderfully refreshing.

The town was in the heart of Raday (Raa-DAY) country and because of the high incidence of leprosy among the Raday tribespeople it was a logical place for the first and largest leprosarium established by The Christian and Missionary Alliance in Vietnam.

The hospital unit was built for in- and out-patient care. The expansive campus included a number of staff houses, both for missionary and national caregivers, plus a chapel. Although operated and staffed largely by Alliance people, over the years the Leprosarium benefited from help extended by the American Leprosy Mission and personnel from the Mennonite Central Committee.

Not all the Leprosarium staff lived on the compound. Some lived in Banmethuot and commuted 10 miles to their work over the less-than-ideal road, now blocked off.

Gail and I sized up the situation. Our Land Rover obviously could not climb over or go around the felled trees. And, if indeed the communists had mined the road, it would not be a very healthy hike.

We decided our best course of action was to drive back into town and talk with the local military. We went first to an American officer.

"Why aren't you checking out things at the Leprosarium?" we asked somewhat impatiently. "There are 30 Americans out there. Why hasn't someone gone out to see about them?"

The officer seemed disinterested. His troops, he informed us, were there to cover military objectives.

"Well," we responded, "we're going out there tomorrow anyway. Our wives are out there and we're going to go get them."

"You're crazy," said the officer.

Gail and I continued the rounds of anyone we thought could help, knocking on every door, trying to motivate the military into action. And why not? Our families were in possible jeopardy. So were more than a score of other Americans. No one seemed to care.

Still weak from the hepatitis and short of sleep, I was exhausted by nightfall. Gail and I finally decided that there was nothing to do but spend another night in town. Come morning we would take matters into our own hands, live or die, survive or perish. We would go to the aid of our wives.

The three large houses occupied by missionaries in Banmethuot were built in a row on a spacious property fronting the highway leading out to the turnoff for the Leprosarium. The houses were about 50 yards back from the road. I was in one of the bedrooms that faced the highway.

Although weary in body I found it hard to sleep. All that night I could hear through the open window the Raday tribal gongs and, of course, the

more typical night sounds we had grown accus-
tomed to, such as crying babies and occasional
gunfire.

I lay down on the bed and prayed for my wife
and sons. It was frustrating not to know what was
happening out there at the Leprosarium. It didn't
help that EG was pregnant. Was all well? Was she
in trouble? Had the Leprosarium been overrun?

I had no answers.

I prayed that God would take care of them. I
prayed that there would be some way we could
keep them all from being harmed by the people
who had felled the trees across the road, the people
who had written the warning, the people who had
threatened to behead anyone who reopened the
road.

It was another long night.

Charlie and EG Long, August 1958.

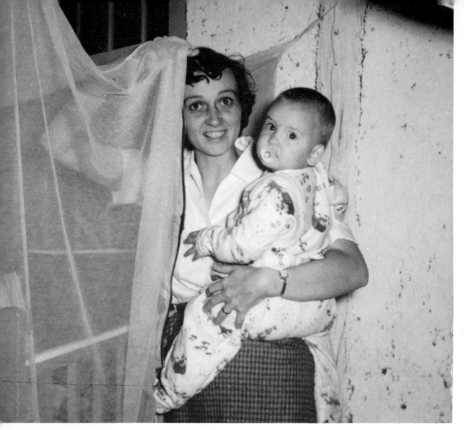

Nathan being put under his "skeeter" at Tra My, 1960.

Xa Bui III apartment extending 100 yards around mountain.

Sung, Mai, Dale Herendeen and Charlie start first survey trip
from Tra My. March, 1960.

EG checks for loss of feeling caused by leprosy.

"Bikers", 1961, Pleiku.

Mip at out-patient clinic.

Beautiful, pre-war Jarai village, 1960.

Jarai village of 155 homes burned by Viet Cong in 1962.

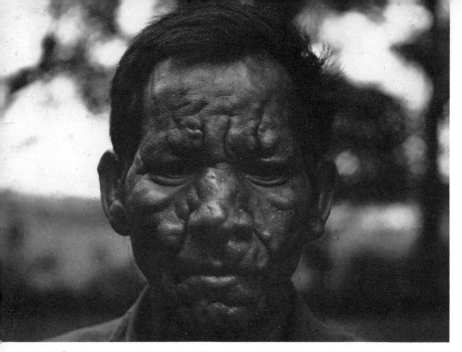

Jarai government worker fired because of leprous appearance.
He later became a Christian and village nurse.

Charlie with "no wasted space" Viet country bus, 1959.

Ga Hao, martyred for Christ, 1961.

Ama Tum preaching at leprosy clinic in 1962; martyred 1970 near Cheo Reo.

Nate, Joby, EG, Charlie, Susie, Ed, 1969.

Rover crosses wood and rope-tied undulating bridge on
Highway 1, the main road between Saigon and Hanoi, 1962.

Rubble of Charlie's office at Pleiku, 1968. The trampled
Gospel of Matthew was retrieved from the rubble on the floor.

Pleiku Bible School sapper bomb damage.

Dr. Ardell Vietti, her assistant and a patient at Leprosarium, 1962.

Marie Ziemer awaits evacuation from
Cam Ranh Bay Military Hospital,
February 1968.

Pleiku Church, 1966.

Charlie and Wing translating in Saigon, 1972.

Military truck destroyed near Catecka Tea Plantation, 1972.

EG prepares Jarai hymbook, Saigon, 1974.

Tribes of Vietnam Field Conference at Dalat, 1960

Front row, L to R:
Lillian Amstutz, Arlene Roseveare, Joyce McNeel, Nancy Josephson, Ellen Duncan, EG Long, Maxine Craig, Tina Schelander, Elizabeth Jackson, Evelyn Mangham, Peggy Argile, Mary Forbes.

Second row L to R:
Myrtle Fune, Helen Evans, Lynne Holiday, Elsie Sloat, Ardel Vietti, Carolyn Griswold, Olive Kingsbury, Betty-Lou Hartson, Ruth Kelk, Jackie Ingram, Bernice Swain, Mildred Ade, Dawn Deets, Irene Fleming.

Third row L to R:
Robert Reed, Richard Philips, Gail Fleming, David Frazier, Ross Duncan, C.G. Ingram, Herb Jackson, Kenneth Swain, Leroy Josephson.

Fourth row L to R:
Jean Fune, Merle Douglas, Gilbert Johnson (guest speaker), Grady Mangham, Charlie Long, Robert Chrisman, Carl Roseveare, Wesley Schelander, Bob McNeel.

Last Field Conference, Dalat, 1974

First row L to R:
Gail Fleming, John Hall, Rick Drummond, Chester Travis, Wesley Schelander, Sr., Grady Mangham, Franklin Irwin, Jack Revelle, Norman Johnson, Bob McNeel, Orrel Steinkamp, Ed Bedford, Richard Phillips.

Second row L to R:
Leroy Josephson, Carol Steckel, Mary Travis, Nancy Josephson, Ginny Steinkamp, Joyce McNeel, Irene Fleming, Agnes Dutton, Unknown, Tina Schelander, Joan Downs, Lillian Philips.

Third row L to R:
Nancy Mack, Joyce Kayser, Elizabeth Heath, Penny Hall, E.G. Long, Cleo Evans, Mary Andrea, Betty Rexilius, Sharon Allwine Bacosmot.

Fourth row L to R:
Keith Kayser, Joan Johnson, Anneke Companjen, Helen Evans, Beth Drummond, Peggy Gunther, Eileen Green, LaDonna Reimer, Faith Bedford, Dawn Deets, Margaret Herron, Evelyn Revelle, Royce Rexilius, Gene Evans.

Fifth row L to R:
Reg Reimer, Elaine Ellison, Harriet Irwin, Bernice Swain, Harold Dutton, John Companjen, Charles Long, Elsie Sloat Douglas, Betty Arnold, Doris Irwin.

Sixth row L to R:
Merle Douglas, Paul Ellison, David Beack, Wesley Schelander, Jr., Ken Swain, Bruce Downs, David Heath, Bob Green, George Irwin.

Oi Wao, the capstone to our ministry in Vietnam. He came to Christ, just before he died, after 14 years of hearing the gospel. "Everybody my age is dead," he said. "I must be 130 years old."

10

The Rescue

From my window I watched the daylight creep across the front yard of the Banmethuot compound and between the long row of large fan palms leading out toward the road.

At the front of the property was a crimson-colored hibiscus hedge. I was still reflecting on the peaceful beauty of the scene when a convoy of Vietnamese marines rumbled past, heading in the direction of the Leprosarium road.

I knew they were marines, the elite troops of the Vietnamese military, because of their particular camouflage color. There must have been 10 or more truckloads of them, all standing at alert.

My spirit soared as I prayed earnestly that they would get out there and find everything all right. With the marines en route it seemed best for Gail and me to await their report before deciding what to do next.

Shortly after noon we received word that the marines had reached the Leprosarium. They had walked most of the way because of the felled trees and the absence of several wooden bridges the VC had burned. The marines had encountered no mines and, best news of all, the Leprosarium compound was secure and all the staff and patients were safe. The notice also said that the road was being put under the control of the regional forces.

Later we learned that the marines, after checking that all the Leprosarium staff were safe, simply departed. Refugees were beginning to report concentrations of communists just beyond the perimeter of the property, but the marines had made no attempt to engage them. They just walked back out to their trucks and returned to town.

As soon as we received the message, Gail and I set out to hike to the Leprosarium. What a happy reunion took place later that afternoon after the uncertainties of the past days faded into only unpleasant memories.

Betty Mitchell had prepared lunch. Archie, her husband, was out trying to clear the road and did not join us. I will never forget eating with Betty and some of the other missionaries on the Mitchells' screened-in porch. It was an oasis of delightful tranquility just before the storm of events so soon to follow.

Now came the task of getting back to Banmethuot.

A large group of Alliance missionaries had been taking an introductory leprosy control course at the Leprosarium. Most had come by plane so they had no vehicles trapped in the jungle. We all assembled to begin the single-file trek.

There was an atmosphere of levity among the group. No one seemed to feel they were in danger. But I had noticed ominous changes in the area and had more serious thoughts on my mind.

Mip and another Raday carried EG's luggage. I followed next with Nathan in one arm and Eddie in the other. Behind me I could hear EG, her thongs flip-flopping against the bottoms of her feet as she walked.

About an hour down the trail through creeks and around felled trees, we reached several army trucks getting ready to return to Banmethuot. I was happy to rest. The walk had been a struggle for me because of the hepatitis.

The soldiers allowed us to climb aboard. The hard steel bed of an army truck is no luxury but it was certainly preferable to walking all the way back into town.

The trail through the forest was one of the world's worst. For most of the way the drivers had the trucks in first gear and four-wheel-drive. Nevertheless, they wasted no time and we all bounced up and down on the steel bed of the truck. It was a very rough trip, especially for EG. But we had little choice.

Even with the "luxury" of the ride, it was evening before we reached Banmethuot and the welcome comfort of the Mission homes.

Seventeen-month-old Eddie awoke the next morning with a high fever. Dr. Vietti, bless her heart, made a special trip by bicycle into town from the Leprosarium to treat him.

I spent the day helping open the Leprosarium road. Dan Gerber, a Mennonite paxman (conscientious objector) doing humanitarian work at the Leprosarium in lieu of military service, was cutting up the trees that the Viet Cong had felled. Once the trunks were cut loose, 40 to 50 loincloth-clad leprosy patients rolled them off the road.

Archie Mitchell and his son Glenn were remov-

ing the thousands of punji (PUN gee) stakes that
the communists had imbedded on the roadway and
shoulders. Punji stakes are short lengths of bamboo
sharpened at both ends. They are pushed into the
ground in clusters, each stake at the same angle.
The exposed tips are coated with manure. Anyone
in a hurry to flee cannot avoid being wounded and
infected by the manure-coated tips.

My job on the road gang was to put rocks in the
creek beds where the still-smouldering bridges had
been burned out. I wrestled the large rocks into the
water, making tracks for the four-wheel-drive
vehicles to ford the creeks. The road was the only
supply route for hundreds of disabled patients. We
had to reopen it.

Wednesday morning EG, Nathan and Eddie and
I took a flight to Pleiku. The Flemings returned in
our Land Rover. That same night, the Viet Cong
entered the Leprosarium compound and took captive Ardel Vietti, Archie Mitchell and Dan Gerber.
They commandeered a Land Rover, forced the
three into it and drove off into the jungle.

The missionary force constantly lived with the
possibility of death. But a spectre more horrible
was capture. Tens of thousands of private citizens
were abducted in those years. Few returned to tell
about it. They simply vanished, leaving widows and
orphans behind.

Months later, the Land Rover was found buried
in the jungle. Its three American occupants were
never heard from.

To this day, Hanoi declares it has no record of
the event.

11

A Ride to Saigon

By the time our flight arrived in Pleiku, EG realized that she was in trouble. The jouncing ride from the Leprosarium into Banmethuot in the back of the army truck had obviously taken its toll.

As quickly as I could I put her on an Air Vietnam flight for Saigon, where fellow missionaries would see that she got medical care. The boys and I remained in Pleiku to await word from the hospital.

The hepatitis had melted 22 pounds from my lanky frame. Still extremely weak, I found myself trying to be both mother and father to two miniature specimens of manhood. Nathan and Eddie played in the red Pleiku dust and mud until they were red-skinned. But at night they scrubbed up clean for their Bible stories and prayer time. They were excited about the new baby Mommy was carrying.

EG and I were excited, too, and for five months we had been anticipating this new arrival. Now those expectations were threatened by the possibility of a miscarriage.

Miscarriage. It was a word I had come to dread.

EG had had two others, the second of them in Vietnam. I had held her hands and tried to help her bear the pain while a Vietnamese doctor had performed the D&C without the benefit of anesthesia. It was fresh on my mind—I had just found the receipt in the drawer.

My love and respect for EG was infinite. She was so strong, so steady, so understanding and empathetic. Now she was facing this present crisis by herself, away from husband and family. At least, if worst came to worst, there would be anesthesia this time.

The news from Saigon was not long in coming. And it was not good.

"You'd better get down here, Charlie," Evelyn Mangham said. "EG is having a miscarriage."

Even though I had considered the possibility, I struggled to absorb Evelyn's words. Obviously EG needed me. Yet it took a great deal of mental effort just to decide what to do. Was it only last March, hardly more than three months ago, that I was a young man of boundless energy? Now it seemed as if I had been exhausted all my life. I struggled to be lucid, logical, competent to do anything.

"Tell EG I'll be there," I told Evelyn.

Meanwhile in Saigon, EG wrote a letter to my folks:

Greetings tonight in the name of our Heavenly Father who loves and cares for us beyond all human measure.

Perhaps you note this is written from Saigon. I flew down last Monday to see the doctor. I was in the hospital for four days and have been at the guest home since. Charlie and the boys are still in Pleiku. I imagine this being his first time alone with them, he has his hands full.

To make a long story short, there isn't going to be an addition to our family now. The doctor did a pregnancy test and I got the report today. It's negative, which means the fetus is dead. So I will stay here until the fetus aborts (miscarries)—which can occur any time.

Needless to say our hearts are sad, yet there is perfect peace that this is His will and that His way is best, though we do not always understand. The Lord's presence and promises have been very precious to my heart at this time and no doubt before you receive this, I shall be ready to return to Pleiku and my boys! How I've missed them this week—all three!

✦ ✦ ✦

With the boys in tow I went out to the American air base at Pleiku and asked for a ride to Saigon. They had a C-123 cargo plane heading that way. They said we could get on it if we wished.

Inside the uninsulated body of the plane were two rows of canvas seats, one row against each side, the passengers facing inward.

The cranking up of the 2,200-horsepower motors terrified Nathan and Eddie, who were strapped in

on either side of me. I looked at each one. Both
were crying their hearts out, but I could hear no
sounds from them above the roar of the engines.
All I could see were their open mouths and the big
tears running down their cheeks.

We finally arrived in Saigon.

EG would surely miscarry. And, added to that,
the communists had just abducted three of our
missionaries—all of them personal friends for
whom we cared deeply. The war was definitely intensifying.

We had been in Vietnam four years. We had one
more to go before our normal furlough. It was the
lowest point in all my years as a missionary.

Just five days after the last letter home, EG wrote
once again:

> No doubt you're anxious to know what
> has happened since I last wrote. I stayed
> here at the home a week and went back to
> see the doctor. We decided to do a D&C
> Friday a.m. so I went to the hospital
> Thursday night. However, during the night I
> "passed" the fetus and placenta so the doc-
> tor decided the operation was not necessary.
>
> For this I praise the Lord. So Wednesday I
> go back for a checkup and can probably go
> back to Pleiku Friday. It will be good to be
> home. Charlie and the boys have been down
> since Tuesday, so it hasn't been nearly so
> lonesome. Eddie is really a character these
> days—so naughty one minute and so sweet
> the next! He seems not as easy to discipline

as Nathan, but in time he'll learn—I hope.

At the Saigon guest house where the boys and I were temporarily staying, I searched out Robert S. Chrisman, then the regional director for Alliance missionary work throughout Asia and the Far East. Himself a former missionary to Thailand, Chrisman could encompass within his big heart the hundreds of missionaries and the dozen or more areas within his administrative responsibility. He could be delightfully humorous at times and equally serious at others. And pensive.

It was evening. Night had already descended on Saigon. I went up to where Mr. Chrisman was standing on the front porch staring off into the night.

"What do you have to do to get a medical furlough?" I asked quietly, not wanting to intrude too forcefully on his reverie.

Perhaps Mr. Chrisman did not hear my question. Perhaps he was lost in his own agony as he thought of Betty Mitchell, robbed of her husband, and the Leprosarium bereaved of three key workers.

Perhaps he was thinking of the nearly 100 Christian and Missionary Alliance missionaries at work in South Vietnam under conditions of war and daily facing the possibility of martyrdom.

Whatever the explanation, Mr. Chrisman did not answer. He just continued to focus on a point far off in the inky distance.

I was angry. Chrisman had not answered me. Was he insensitive to what was happening to EG and me? I found that hard to comprehend. I knew him, both by personal contact and reputation, to be otherwise.

I often wonder what course our lives might have taken had he answered, had he offered us the option of going home right then.

But there was no answer.

We stayed.

12

Ambushed!

I was a long time getting my full strength back. Although it was eight months before I really felt well again, I continued to do the work the Lord had called me to do in and around Pleiku.

Bob and Bobbie Reed had worked in the Cheo Reo (CHAY-oh RAY-oh) valley for a full term with the Jarai people and were on furlough in the United States. I was expected to cover their station while they were away. They, too, held leprosy clinics monthly. From July 1962 to July 1963 I would travel the Cheo Reo road many times.

Soon I began to know every bump, hole, rock and normal hazard. Usually someone wanted to go with me. The uninsulated cab of that noisy Rover often became a classroom to teach many lessons. It was in that two-seat environment that I admonished Brao not to hate the Vietnamese for killing his brother, Ga Hao, but to cause blessing to flow from the tragedy by bringing all the Jarai to heaven with him.

Many times I said in Brao's hearing, "We can reach all 200,000 Jarai in our lifetime for Christ." One day, as we drove along, he suddenly had a great thought. Turning toward me, he said, "Mr. Long, we can reach all 200,000 of the Jarai for Christ in my lifetime."

"Wow, that's a great idea, Brao," I responded. "Let's do it."

◆ ◆ ◆

It was about 25 kilometers along the valley floor to the base of Red Mountain from where the road rises 1,800 feet in just 70 kilometers (about 42 miles).

Lik (LEEK) sat in the middle with Kreal (CREE aal) on the right by the door. The windows were open and the rear canvas was rolled up in an effort to get some cross ventilation. We picked up a young, black-pajama-clad Vietnamese hitchhiker. He jumped into the back of the truck behind Kreal.

Bamboo thickets formed columns on either side of the road. The wheels churned up billows of red dust behind us. Kreal always slept in the car, his head bobbing like a swivel. Lik sat stiffly, eyes ahead, alert, watching. The hitchhiker was also watching intently so he could let me know where to drop him off.

The road was cut into the mountain, the hillside rising on my left, the valley descending abruptly on the far side. Bamboo thickets formed a kind of elongated skylight above us.

Suddenly I thought, *What would I do if we were ambushed?* Feeling that such an event was a distinct possibility in this type of terrain, I instantly began to plan my strategy. *If they attack from the front, I* reasoned, *I will brake and dive into the ditch to get away from the target—the car. If they attack from the side, with so much dust being raised by the Rover, I will just keep going. If they attack from the rear, I will keep going, using the dust as a cover.*

Rrack. Rrack. Rrack. Pop. Pop. Pop. Pop.

"Bullets!" I shouted.

I ducked low to the right. Acting on instinct from my private strategy-planning session only a few minutes earlier, I shifted into third and plunged the pedal to the floor. The vehicle surged forward. The hitchhiker dove onto the floor. Lik focused on the direction of the gunfire. Kreal's head jerked as his eyes blinked open. All I could see behind me was a huge cloud of red dust.

The thought flashed through my mind: *Those shots came from ARVN* (South Vietnamese government forces) *playing with us!* It made me mad. I wanted to go back and get whoever had fired at us. *Not a good idea,* I decided. *He still has a gun!*

I roared off and came upon some ARVN soldiers about two kilometers down the road. I braked hard, stopping next to a sergeant standing on the shoulder.

"Do you have any troops back there?" I asked somewhat hotly.

"No, we are all here," he said.

The hitchhiker jumped out and ran up to the sargeant.

"Oh, sergeant, sergeant!" he erupted. "The Viet Cong shot us back there. Too scary! Too scary! I can't stop shaking!"

I dropped the gearshift into first and drove on. I

was still angry. Nobody slept the rest of that deserted road home. And there weren't even any marks on the Rover to prove to my colleagues that I had really been shot at!

A jungle rumor later revealed that a Viet Cong "had shot and killed God." Thankfully the report was exaggerated!

That night, as EG welcomed me home and we embraced, I was suddenly overwhelmed by how close I had come to not seeing her again on earth. It shook me up.

But there was a note awaiting me. It was from Chil (CHEEL), a Christian from out near the Cambodian border. His baby daughter had died. Would I please come and have a Christian burial for his baby? My stomach did a few flipflops at the thought. I decided to sleep on it.

The next morning dawned bright and beautiful. *Let's do it!* I said to myself. *Chil would do it for me.* So I headed the 55 kilometers to the border.

Past the tea plantations, small scrub forest covered the countryside. *Lots of cover here for the VC to use for an ambush,* I mused. *This road is Danger Inc.*

By about ten o'clock I swung to the right and down an ungraded trail into the woods and to Chil's house. The government had forced the villagers to move to a more secure area on the opposite side of the road from their former village.

People gathered around the vehicle as I pulled to a stop. The little girl's body was lying in a hand-hewn casket, still in the round form of a tree.

I thought of the story Mip had told me during

one of our many forays into the countryside. He and his twin brother were born in this same village. His mother and the twin died during the birth. Since Mip's father could not feed a newborn baby, he laid Mip on top of his mother's casket and began to shovel in the dirt to bury his baby alive. Fortunately, an aunt who was nursing rescued Mip and became his mother.

We carried the casket to the small church Chil had built in the village. Chil's first wife and all seven of their children had died of disease. In those pre-Christian days he had offered a buffalo sacrifice for each of them, an act which had impoverished him. But now he was a new man in Christ.

I told the small gathering how Jesus loved little children and how we needed to become like them to be saved. We sang "Jesus Loves Me." Some received Christ.

Then we took the tiny casket to the Rover. I rolled back the canvas and the truck bed was soon filled with mourners. With so many people standing and holding on to the frame I crept back up the trail to the main road and down to the cemetery in the old village.

I committed the body to the red soil to await the resurrection and we sang "Only Trust Him." Everyone helped to put the pile of dirt into the grave and we all crawled back into the truck—at least 20 of us.

Back home about suppertime it felt so good to be cool and to be with EG, Nathan and Eddie. The events of the day made me appreciate them all the more.

About a year later I met Chil in Pleiku. By then he was a refugee, forced from his village by the hostilities.

"Oi (Grandfather)," he said, "do you remember the day you came out and buried my little girl?"

I remembered it well.

"Yes," I said. "I do."

"Well, that morning," Chil went on, "two Viet Cong came through our village carrying a Browning automatic rifle. I saw them going up toward the road. 'What are you going to do?' I asked them. They said, 'We're going up on the road and shoot cars today.'

"I said, 'Don't shoot our missionary. He's coming out here this morning to bury my baby. He doesn't work for the government or the army. Don't shoot him.' "

The trip flashed through my mind—I had driven through the sights of that Browning automatic rifle four times that day!

"That night," he continued, "when the Viet Cong walked through the village they said to me, 'We were good to you today. We didn't shoot your missionary!' " That, despite the fact that mine was the only car that passed their vantage point the whole day!

So on back-to-back days, Friday and Saturday, November 2 and 3, 1962, my life was spared. I *know* of those two times. There may have been many others. Only God knows.

"Dear Ma and Pa," I wrote June 5, just before furlough time, "we are selling all our old stuff and hoping to get some new things. I am turning my car over to its new owner tomorrow after 83,000 kilometers (60,000) miles and no bullet holes. There were times when I wondered if I would ever see home again but now I feel it is more possible that we shall get home in one piece. Forty-seven days from tonight we will sleep in Charlotte, Lord willing."

✦ ✦ ✦

In October 1962 the United States Air Force deployed a second air division to Vietnam. And early in 1963 the South Vietnamese Army suffered its first major defeat.

A month later a United States Senate panel reported 12,000 U.S. troops in Vietnam on what it termed "dangerous assignment." In May, Buddhists within Vietnam began what would stretch into four months of demonstrations, revolts and self-immolations.

When the time for our first furlough finally arrived in July, EG and I looked forward to a year of respite from the tensions of a country at war.

But as we boarded our flight for America we wondered just what kind of a South Vietnam would be there when we returned in a year's time.

13

"Pray for the Jarai"

When we left Vietnam for furlough in 1963, we took with us 400 bookmarks woven by Jarai tribeswomen. Each one said, "Pray for the Jarai." In the churches we visited we gave a bookmark to anyone who promised to pray *daily* for our people.

In North Carolina two women led the charge in praying for us and the Jarai. Janie Hargrave, a Presbyterian from Lumberton, kept the women of that area praying for us. The other woman was Ally Devenish, an Alliance Bible teacher from Asheville. In 1959 Mrs. Devenish was asked to begin a Bible study in Charlotte for a group that had been founded by Morrow Graham, Billy Graham's mother, among others.

Mrs. Devenish rode a circuit by bus from Asheville to Greenville to Charlotte every week. My parents attended her class in Charlotte, a group which grew to over 150. The group was mighty in prayer and responded to our frequent and urgent appeals. The spiritual and physical wars were parallel and real. Prayer was our heavy, long-range artillery. A press release on August 16, 1963 reported that there were only four established churches and 500 Christians among the Jarai. The passion of our furlough year was to beg people to pray for the Jarai.

While we were busy in homeland churches, the war in Vietnam was escalating by the day. On August 21, President Ngo Dinh Diem ordered an attack by the military on Buddhist pagodas believed to be harboring communist subversives.

On November 1, a military coup toppled the government. The following day President Diem and his brother were both assassinated.

Twenty days later John F. Kennedy was also assassinated and Lyndon B. Johnson succeeded him as president.

On February 7, 1964, Johnson ordered the withdrawal from Vietnam of all American dependents. In April, North Vietnam, which until then had relied on an ample supply of sympathizers in the South and its own corps of cadres, began infiltrating regular army units into South Vietnam.

In June we wrote:

> Our year of furlough from South Vietnam is nearly finished and in a few short weeks we will be winging our way across the broad Pacific back to the front lines.
>
> God called us to Vietnam in 1958. We believe He is sending us back to Vietnam now. We are going back into danger, back into the sufferings of the people, back into a land needful of the love and compassion of the Living Christ. Not one single thing that

we can think of will be easy during the next
five-year term. We must be filled by the
Holy Spirit to meet the challenge. Can we
trust you to pray for us during the next five
years? It is not enough for our nation to
send aid money and troops to save Vietnam.
We must call on God, Who is sovereign, to
halt the drives of the enemy and to preserve
Vietnam as a free nation.

After 12 months of furlough we would return to
an increasingly bloody war.

In July, 1964, EG, Nathan, six, Eddie, four, and
five-month-old Amelia Susan—Susie—and I wing-
ed our way back to South Vietnam. On the Hong
Kong-Saigon leg of the trip, enjoying the lounge of
the Cathay Pacific Lockheed Electra, I caught
sight of the steel gray reflective waters of the Gulf
of Tonkin below us.

Suddenly, the fun, the excitement, were gone. I
knew danger lay ahead, mostly for me, but also for
my family. Since 1961 EG had purposely not gone
out into the villages. In case I "got it," the kids
would at least have one parent, we rationalized.

Oh, Lord, I prayed, *I rest on Isaiah 8:13 again:
"Sanctify the* LORD *of hosts himself; and let him be your
fear, and let him be your dread" (KJV). Lord, here we
go again! Let me fear only You.*

Less than a month later, the U.S. Navy, in
response to an attack from gunboats in the Gulf of
Tonkin, made retaliatory air strikes against selected
military targets in the North. On August 7 Con-
gress passed the Tonkin Gulf Resolution. America

was now in an undeclared air war on North Vietnam. To declare war would have forced the communist bloc to declare war on the U.S., possibly
the Third World War.

What until that time had been a relatively small
war, abetted by Chinese aid to North Vietnam and
American aid to South Vietnam, now had all the
markings of a full-blown conflagration.

Up country in Pleiku we could sense the
heightened tension. Political turmoil, social upheaval
and unpredictable and often deadly military action
became commonplace. Frankly, we expected South
Vietnam to fall. And it probably would have, had it
not been for the arrival of American combat forces
in 1965—the Big Build-Up.

EG and I, however, were not in Vietnam to fight
a war or even to be a commentary on the war. We
were there to see that the Jarai tribespeople were
evangelized and to build the Church of Jesus
Christ among them.

Ever since my years at Toccoa Falls College I had
sensed a God-given obligation—I felt it that strong-
ly—to translate the Scriptures into another language.

During our first years at Pleiku I had dabbled at
translation work but quickly realized I was not yet
ready. Experience in the Jarai language (or any other
for that matter) could only be bought with time.

A Vietnamese missionary, Rev. Pham Xuan Tin
(Faam Swan TEEN), had been the first to reach
the Jarai with the good news of Jesus Christ. Both
Mr. Tin and his wife were small, fragile-looking
people, hardly the type to be riding horseback
throughout the southern highlands around Pleiku.

Mr. Tin had translated the four Gospels and Acts into Jarai and the British and Foreign Bible Society had printed them as separate books.

Like most initial translations done under time pressure, they would later need improvement. But at least the Jarai had some written Scriptures.

Rev. and Mrs. Truong van Sang (TrueAANG VANG SHAANG) replaced the Tins in 1951. They were from the southern delta area of Vietnam, where the culture was as remote from the Jarai as mine was. Pastor Sang, as he was called, continued to translate the Scriptures, while others of us were trying to bring the Jarai to Christ so they would want those Scriptures. The passion to reach real live people always hindered the more scholarly work of translation. Neither of us was making much headway.

If language familiarity was essential to a good translation of the Scriptures—and it was—then my first order of business was to become fluent in Jarai. I decided to make our 1964-68 term a time for nurturing my knowledge of the language.

I preached in Jarai. I taught in Jarai. I talked in Jarai.

Preaching and teaching during those years of war were tough. We were sowing the seed, sowing the seed, sowing the seed, but not always seeing results. We felt a sense of impatience. Jesus at one point said to His disciples, "As long as it is day, we must do the work of him who sent me. Night is coming, when no one can work" (John 9:4).

We were working intensely to sow the seed among the Jarai, but we could sense that night was approaching. Would darkness descend over South Vietnam before we could reap a harvest?

The question both haunted and drove us. Time seemed to be fast running out. All we could ask was that people would pray for us and for the Jarai.

14

Crises at Pleiku

During the early 60s the South Vietnamese government, with assistance from the United States, had resettled thousands of impoverished and usually illiterate lowland Vietnamese into the central highlands which had been traditionally claimed by the tribespeople.

They bulldozed clearings in the jungle, then laid out towns complete with market, government buildings, Catholic church and sites for rows of thatched homes.

Once the town was established they trucked 500 to 1000 people up from the lowlands, assigning each person or family a piece of land to work. They were to plant rice, rubber, kenaf (cultivated for its fiber) and other designated crops. Obviously this vast effort at social engineering brought great changes to the highlands.

The Mission assigned Franklin Irwin (George's younger brother) the task of establishing churches in those villages.

Le Thanh (Lay TAAN) was the westernmost resettlement village. I had assisted in the development of the Tin Lanh Church in the town and had taught and preached there numerous times. I had also made friends with the district chief, a decorated captain of the Vietnam Army.

In June, 1965, Le Thanh was overrun by the Viet Cong. When the news got out, a relief convoy of provincial troops went to the rescue. Horns blared and citizen soldiers came running from all directions as the convoy formed in the streets of Pleiku. The men pulled on their olive drab shirts and wives chased after them with forgotten gear.

"Hurry up!" the sergeant yelled. "Get in the trucks!"

The ruff puffs bounced, bumped and swayed from side to side as the Toyotas agonized single file like mechanical elephants down the main street of Pleiku and up the long grade to the junction of Route 19. This was a highway that ran like a belt around the middle of South Vietnam from the sea to Cambodia—a possible line for cutting the country in half.

The U.S. advisor's jeep was first in the column, followed by a patrol of the ruff puffs scouring the road and woods along the base of the mountain to the left and up through the narrow pass. There was no sign of the VC.

"Back to the trucks," the sergeant yelled again. "No VC here." The patrol returned to the trucks and the engines began to crank to life.

Then suddenly, flames and smoke from a B-40 rocket engulfed the lead jeep. Then mortars plummeted from the sky onto the last truck in the column. The rest of the vehicles were caught between the two stricken vehicles.

Rockets and mortars continued but the real ter-

ror came out of the rice paddies on both sides of
the road. The VC had lain unseen, camouflaged,
waiting until the patrol searched the wrong place
and returned off guard.

The radio operator called, "Who hears, please
help. We are trapped beyond Catacka. We'll all be
killed. All dead."

Two U.S. military advisors in the convoy were killed.

When helicopter-borne Raday Eagle troops tried
to rescue the provincial troops, they were met with
37-millimeter anti-aircraft fire—a significant up-
surge in firepower. The communists had clearly
come to Le Thanh to stay.

Pastor Tan somehow managed to escape from
the town and made his way to Pleiku where he
sought me out. Some days later, when reports indicated decreased fighting, Pastor Tan asked me if he
should return to his village.

How do you advise a man who faces the possibility of death no matter which way he turns? He
and I agreed that we would pray about the matter
overnight.

The following morning he was excited. I could tell
instinctively that he had arrived at a decision.

"My place as the shepherd is with my sheep," he
said simply.

We prayed together and shook hands. Then he
was gone—back to his ministry among the
believers in Le Thanh.

Days later I learned that Pastor Tan had been
murdered by the communists. They had pitched his
body by the side of the road. Some of his congregation found the body and buried it.

I was very angry at the news of Pastor Tan's death. It took me years to understand at least in part what seemed, in this case and others, to be such senseless loss and tragedy.

Concerned that the fighting might reach Pleiku, I sent EG, Eddie and Susie out of harm's way to Dalat, a sort of neutral Switzerland respected by all sides in the war. Nathan, by then seven, was in the second grade at school in Bangkok.

(I need to explain about the Dalat School. The school began in February 1929 with eight students. Herbert and Lydia Jackson, Alliance missionaries working in Cantho, were sent to Dalat to supervise construction of a two-story dormitory with six bedrooms. Over the years it expanded to become a regional school serving Alliance missionaries in all of Southeast Asia. After the terrorists' bombing of the U.S. embassy in Saigon, Lyndon Johnson ordered American dependents to leave the country. Because of the risk, the school was moved first to Bangkok, then in 1965 to Malaysia. But it continued, and continues, to be called the Dalat School.)

When the Le Thanh fighting threatened a Special Forces camp, South Vietnam threw some of its best units into the fray. The Viet airborne brigade and the Viet marines came to the rescue.

A young American captain, H. Norman Schwarzkopf, was the U.S. advisor to the airborne brigade. Again VC mortars caught the troops exposed on the rocky roadbed of Route 19. Twelve Marines died from one shell blast.

Pinned by the crossfire, they were forced to stay on the road. As an American advisor stood by an armored personnel carrier consulting a map with his Vietnamese counterpart, a B-40 rocket whooshed at the APC but struck the American officer. The explosion killed all the standing men.

But there was something in this series of battles of greater significance to me. The last rescue party to come to the aid of western Pleiku province was an all-American unit, the 173rd Airborne. It was the first time I had seen American combat units in the fighting.

I knew that construction had been progressing on a new runway at Pleiku. One night I heard the whistling roar of incoming C-130 cargo planes. In a 30-minute period the whole 173rd Airborne landed on that unfinished runway. They quickly moved west on Route 19 to back up the hard-pressed Vietnamese units.

The big American war was beginning. In another month, two more large battles would be fought along the south side of Route 19, just a few miles east of the Ho Chi Minh Trail.

As the fighting continued, more than 200 bodies of Vietnamese provincial soldiers were trucked back to Pleiku for their widows to identify and bury. Wails and crying filled the air, along with ghastly diesel fumes. Women clasped handtowels over their faces, fear distorting their countenances as they searched for husband, son, brother, father, uncle.

Cries of "Dead already! Daddy's dead! Life is too miserable!" filled the air.

Women collapsed in heaps on the ground in unbridled grief. Some would plunge themselves into the lake to escape their pain. Simple wooden caskets were brought to begin the burial process.

There is no doubt in my mind that the arrival of American combat troops saved Pleiku. The war situation, so seemingly hopeless only days before their arrival, now took on new optimism.

With the area seemingly secured, my family returned from their brief exile at Dalat. Perhaps after all I would realize my dream of translating the Scriptures into Jarai. Every day in Pleiku brought me that much closer to the time when my fluency in Jarai would permit me to try.

I could hardly wait.

✦ ✦ ✦

Little by little my Jarai improved. I was speaking it constantly.

Your glottis works forever in Jarai. Your throat gets more and more tired and your mouth drier and drier, especially in the dry season when humidity is low and there is smoke from the burning of vegetation.

And dust! During dry season I have seen nine inches of dust on the road! You can hear it, just like flour, churning up from the wheels of your car.

In our second term we had a VW double-cabin pickup with the typical Volkswagon rear engine. Some mornings I put fresh oil in its oil bath air filter and by evening had to use a screwdriver to dig out the concentration of dust and oil before replenishing it for the next day's drive.

Mixing with workmen and suppliers on building projects improved both my Jarai and Vietnamese.

At Pleiku alone during those four years I was involved in 16 or 17 building projects ranging from churches to missionary homes to warehouses to a permanent new leprosy clinic.

In the course of all those projects, we experienced many miracles. There was, for instance, the time we needed steel reinforcing rods (rebar) for the concrete columns to support a church roof. The pastor and I paid a visit to the local Chinese merchant.

Yes, he had the rebar we needed. He did some calculating on his abacus and announced he could sell it to us for $1,000. We did not have $1,000. The fact was we did not have any money. Inflation had taken away the value of any money we might have had.

"It's for a church," the pastor said. "Can you give us a discount?"

"A church?" rasped the merchant in a haughty voice. "What is a church?" Clearly he was not about to make any concession on his steel, especially for a church.

We left disheartened.

In Pleiku there was an American International Development Agency official. Whenever I encountered him around town he always delighted in reminding me that he was an atheist.

I walked into this man's office that afternoon on other business.

"Hey, Long," he called before I could say a word. "Could you use some rebar?"

Could I use some rebar! I tried to disguise my surprise and enthusiasm.

"What size?" I asked as matter-of-factly as I could.

He told me. The steel, left over from a bridge project, was exactly the size, quantity and length we were shopping for, and this American who claimed not to believe in God was offering it to me free. I could hardly believe what I was hearing.

"Just sit on it!" I said, "I'll be back in 15 minutes with a truck."

✦ ✦ ✦

Our house was filled with guests during these years and our table served colonels, privates, church leaders, world travelers, visiting wives of local Americans, reporters, engineers and embassy officials.

One evening about dusk a young Vietnamese appeared at the door wearing a tan trench coat. He looked like a caricature of a western spy. He said he had been assigned to guard us for the night and showed me a .38 pistol in his coat pocket.

A bit suspicious, I went to our bedroom and returned with my shotgun.

"I really don't think we need you," I said. "This shotgun will kill a tiger as far away as the front gate." As I talked I noisily rammed shells in and out of the chamber.

"Since no one belongs inside our gates at night after they are locked," I continued, "I just run this thing out the window and 'boom.' I really appreciate your offer, but I wouldn't want you to get hurt in my yard."

He decided to leave. I never did find out which side he was on but I felt better that he was not there.

✦ ✦ ✦

On October 13, 1966, EG gave birth to Joanna Elizabeth. We nicknamed her Joby. Travel being not especially safe in 1966, Joby was born in the metal leprosy clinic building near our house on the Pleiku compound.

Joby rounded out our family: two boys—Nathan and Eddie, and two girls—Susie and Joby. I could not have been more proud.

✦ ✦ ✦

Night and day we heard gunfire, cannons, mortars, choppers, planes, bombs and the buh-bah-buh-bah-buh-bah—BOOM of carpet bombing by high-flying B-52s. Many people we knew were killed. Frankly, I myself did not expect to survive.

Through preaching, teaching, providing medical treatment in the villages and interacting with Jarai people in the normal work-a-day world of the villages and the abnormal world of war, my language skills were being honed for the day when I could seriously begin the translation of the New Testament and Psalms into idiomatic, understandable Jarai.

As 1967 drew to a close, we could not foresee that in less than a month an event would occur that would forever alter international history as well as missionary activity in Southeast Asia.

15

Tet 1968

For those involved in the Vietnam War—and that includes a whole generation of Americans—Tet 1968 will be forever etched in their minds. For sure, Tet 1968 is indelibly stamped on the mind of every missionary serving in Vietnam at that time.

At Tet, people of the Orient lay aside normal responsibilities to celebrate the advent of a new year. It is a time of merriment and relaxation. Tet '68—beginning Monday, January 29—was anything but that. The communists chose that precise time for their surprise offensive.

Our family had already bought tickets for Saigon. Nathan and Eddie would be leaving there on Saturday for school in Malaysia. After seeing the boys off EG, Susie, Joby and I would fly on up to Nhatrang to spend a week of vacation with Spence and Barbara Sutherland.

Spence taught at the seminary. Their home overlooked the "Kiss Your Husband" Bay on the clear-blue South China Sea. Barb and Spence had children about the same age as ours. Barb would be the ultimate Southern California hostess—hammocks hanging on their breezy porches, the aroma of freshly baked oat bread following the breezes.

Spence and I would swim the bay together and I would unload my war stories on him. I really needed a vacation. 1967 had been a busy year with the construction and funding of the Pleiku Leprosy Center. It had also been emotionally draining.

For three and a half years the gunfire had never stopped. Explosions were the static background noise of our lives. Quiet was always threatening. Yes, a week at the beach was just what we needed.

The Air Vietnam office was a near mob scene when I went to reconfirm our tickets. I've never seen so many people in one small space. All were pushing, wheedling, begging to buy seats out of Pleiku. Maybe it was just the excitement over the holiday. But I had seen Tet come and go many times. Something was different. People were offering big money to get out of Pleiku.

Three or four Jarai came to our house Thursday afternoon and asked if they could take coffee leaves off our trees. It was an unusual request. I asked them why they needed coffee leaves.

"We're going to have a funeral in our village," they explained. "For the feast that follows we will use the leaves as plates."

Using leaves for plates was a customary Jarai practice. Coffee leaves are fairly large and waxen, similar to magnolia leaves in the American South. But the Jarai normally got their "plates" from the forest, where the leaves were even larger.

"Don't you have better leaves out in the jungle?" I asked.

"Yes," they answered, "but we can't go out there right now because the forest is full of the enemy."

"What do you mean, 'full of the enemy'?" I pressed.

"There are literally thousands of communist soldiers out there," the men went on to explain. "They all have new rifles, new equipment. We do not think we should go out to the forest just now to get leaves."

I gave the men permission to gather leaves from our trees, but as soon as they had left I got in the car and drove the short distance to the home of our city pastor.

As the two of us stood talking we could see the village where the leaf-gatherers lived.

"If the people in that village were to go into the jungle to get leaves to use as plates," I posed, "where would they go?"

The pastor pointed to a trail. From where the two of us were standing we could see the area. *So, if the communists are in there,* I thought, *they could be in Pleiku within 10 minutes!*

Then I knew. The Jarai had come to get leaves, true. But they were also subtly warning me of danger. They were saying in effect, "Get out while you can. It's time for you to leave!"

If the message needed reinforcement, it came that evening with a visit from some American military personnel.

"You need to get out of Pleiku," they said flatly. They had just interrogated some captured communists who had boasted, "There's no way you can defeat us. We're going to beat you now—tonight!"

It was ominous news.

"We're booked to leave tomorrow at noon," I told the Americans. "Is that soon enough?"

"That should be okay," they replied.

As it was, the report was only too accurate. We were awakened about three a.m. by communist mortar fire directed at Camp Holloway about three miles east of us. EG and I jumped out of bed and ran to the front of the house. As we stepped into the yard one of the salvos hit an ammunition dump at the camp. Five thousand tons of ammunition exploded in a fireball that reddened the sky and silhouetted the trees and intervening homes.

The Americans and South Vietnamese answered with artillery. For the rest of the night the duel continued. Normally the Americans directed their gunfire away from the town so as not to endanger any of the townspeople. This time they had turned their guns and were firing right over Pleiku to where the communists troops were launching their mortar attack.

Despite the military action we were able to fly out on schedule Friday afternoon. Again, there was near panic at Air Vietnam. Dave and Jeannie Frazier, also living in Pleiku, had managed to book a Friday U.S. government flight out as well. Their flight was canceled.

✦ ✦ ✦

Siesta time always kept Saigon behind closed doors. No one in their right mind was out in the noonday sun unless, of course, you count passengers who have just stepped of a plane at Tan-son-nhut (Taang Shuhng NHOOK) Airport. That was us.

The missionary guest home at 329 Vo-tanh was fully occupied with missionaries and their school-bound offspring. The kids were happy to see their friends, show off war booty and chase the scamper-ing transparent lizards that ate little bugs on the walls. There was lots of hugging and loud greetings as adults from all over South Vietnam got together.

The missionaries of Vietnam loved each other and always looked forward to getting together for these send-off times. The next 24 hours would be sweet and sour—sweet to see old friends, sour to farewell the kids for a four-month semester at Dalat School.

Conversations always turned to two subjects: "How is the church doing in your area?" and "How is the war where you are?"

Saturday morning Marie Ziemer and Ruth Thompson asked me to go to Air Vietnam to change their flight to Banmethuot from Monday (Tet eve) to Sunday, so that they could be home to prepare for all the guests they would have during the Tet week.

On the first day of Tet families stay at home, but the rest of the week is for visiting. Everyone dresses in their best clothes and makes the rounds of all their friends.

"Don't go back," I urged the women. "Call Bob (Ziemer) and Ed (Thompson) and have them come here. Something really big is going to happen on the plateau. I expect they will hit Kontum, Pleiku and Banmethuot.

"Aw, Charlie," Marie responded, "we have to go back. Everyone expects us to be there. We will have so much company. Besides, the VC have called a truce for Tet."

Not easily put off, I pleaded, "Let me call Bob. There won't be a truce. It's just another ruse. Pleiku had a bad night Thursday and I expect more."

Marie told me there had been a recent bold VC assault in downtown Banmethuot also. The area had been dangerous for over nine years now. Although they were afraid, the women insisted on returning.

Against my good judgment I went downtown to Air Vietnam and rebooked their tickets for Sunday, January 28.

Saturday afternoon we waved our children off to school through wet eyes hidden behind sun glasses. The guest home was much quieter that night and now the serious conversations about the war began.

I had been telling war stories for years and was sometimes accused of being pessimistic. But we lived in the provinces and were privy to information the missionaries in the city did not always hear.

Monday morning, Tet eve, EG, Susie, Joby and I happily boarded our flight for Nhatrang. It was a DC-6B plane with a nice lounge at the back, just where our seats happened to be. A group of French tourists heading for the beach surrounded us as I pointed out some landmarks on the ground. I was feeling great—ready for some R and R and free of responsibility for a while.

We glided in over the idyllic blue waters and beach of Nhatrang. Spence met us at the airport and we were soon headed north across the river bridge, along the palm-lined road by the beach. Bougainvillea bloomed purple and white. Papaya trees grew in the yards.

We finally arrived at the Sutherlands'. *What a beautiful place to be after the dust-covered world of Pleiku,* I thought. *Everything is so-o-o clean!* I was in a bathing suit in a flash. It was wonderful.

About midnight, long chains of firecrackers began to explode serially in the fishing village near-by. Then, prroop, prroop, prroop.

AK-47s! *Their* weapons!

I sat straight up in bed. At Pleiku I could judge where and what was happening by the sounds of the different weapons and whether it was friendly or unfriendly fire. Here in Nhatrang I didn't know what was going on.

A 50-caliber machine gun answered the AKs. I could tell by the sound that the machine guns hadn't moved. The VC were attacking a fixed in-stallation. As the firing intensified I reached over to EG. Her body was stiff. I reassured her that there was nothing to fear—at least not yet. *You've got to know when to panic,* I thought to myself. *If you panic too early, then you have no strength to panic when you need to!*

We prayed.

Out in the living room I found Spence standing in the dark, looking out the back of the house. We could see flashes toward town. We stepped out into the white sandy driveway behind his house and watched the firing.

In the half light, some time later, I made out some shadows coming from the school down the drive behind a neighboring house. When they got to within 100 feet or so I was able to make out the shape of a helmeted soldier leading a column of uniformed men. His weapon was pointed at the ground about 10 feet in front of him.

Many times the VC had captured and worn ARVN uniforms to deceive people. We stood still as they approached. The weapon stayed pointed ahead. I saw a toothy smile in front of us. They were friendlies! I began to pray for our associates in Kontum, Pleiku and Banmethuot. If the VC were attacking Nhatrang, usually thought of as a relatively safe area, what was it like there?

I sat on the back stoop at daybreak, listening to the constant gunfire coming from the center of town. A Douglas twin-engined C-47 droned overhead from the ocean. I watched as it tipped up its right wing and unleashed the fire of three Gatling guns. I rubbed my eyes. *I must be seeing things,* I thought.

The Armed Forces Radio and Television Network began to report the news. The attacks were nationwide. General Westmoreland himself talked to the troops over the air. It was not clear who was winning. I kept saying, "He's been caught with his pants down."

Spence and I went across the ridge to the Catholic Seminary to get a better view of what was happening in the city. Rockets plunged into the provincial headquarters. Korean troops swarmed up the beach toward the building. Choppers removed wounded from the beach.

A bullet dinged a tin roof beside our heads. We ducked down into a dry fish pond and peeked over the edge, praying all the while. I was very concerned for our colleagues in Pleiku and the Christians of the area. I thanked the Lord for sparing EG and the kids from whatever was happening there.

The next few days passed slowly as the fighting continued and we hunkered down with the Sutherlands.

Then, the news.

16

Banmethuout

Late Friday evening, February 2, Far East Broadcasting Company Radio Manila reported that all our missionary colleagues in Banmethuout—except Marie Ziemer and Carolyn Griswold—had been killed or captured. Marie and Carolyn, they said, had been evacuated to the Nhatrang Military Hospital.

We were stunned, overwhelmed with the finality of the report. Our beloved colleagues—gone, murdered, martyred. When the initial shock began to abate, our thoughts turned toward Marie and Carolyn across town in the hospital, in what condition we did not know.

Four of us jumped into an ancient Morris Minor and headed for the hospital. National Highway 1 was completely deserted, not even a horse cart, bus, bike or pedestrian. It was scary, ominous, unnerving.

Burt Houck, the driver, stopped the car and looked around at all of us.

"Do you want me to go on?" he asked. We all agreed to go on.

The old car was not low and sleek. I felt very exposed. The only thing moving was us!

We were stopped at several military check points along the way. The troops came up out of deep bunkers to check our IDs. Some were Korean, some Vietnamese, but all were keeping their heads down low. At the hospital we heard the news that Carolyn had died in surgery. We were ushered in to see Marie. Petite, beautiful Marie. She looked so out of place in the stark surrounding of the military hospital. Her hair was white, her porcelain skin sutured in 18 places with black thread.

Tearless and emotionless, she told us about the recent events at Banmethuot.

"We heard the shooting in the middle of the night," Marie began. "Then we heard a huge explosion. We thought that maybe one of the government tanks had been hit by a rocket. Bob looked out and saw that the Griswold house had been blown up.

"At daylight he and Ed (Thompson) dug through the wreckage and found Carolyn badly hurt and her father, Leon Griswold, dead. They brought them to the servants' quarters behind our house. Ruth (Wilting) and Betty (Olsen) tried to treat Carolyn. Because VC were all around and bullets were flying, they couldn't get her to the hospital.

"Wednesday morning the men dug out the garbage pit and made it into a bunker. Late Wednesday evening the VC blew up the Thompson house and later that night the fighting got so bad that we left the servants' quarters, ran through gunfire and got down in the bunker.

"At daylight Thursday Ruth and Betty went to get medicine for Carolyn. While they were gone our house was blown apart. North Vietnamese came from everywhere. Bob decided to go out with his hands raised but they shot him in the head and chest. He fell over a clothesline.

"Ruth came running to the bunker with bullets flying around her. She fell into the bunker praying, 'Lord, help me so I can help the others.' Betty was not with her.

"Ed raised his hands and asked for mercy. They either shot him or a grenade got us all. Ed, his wife, Ruth, and Ruth Wilting were killed in the bunker. The soldiers made me come out and took me prisoner with Betty Olsen, Hank Blood and Mike Benge. A young Raday man helped me escape and got me to the hospital. They brought Carolyn and me here by chopper."

We stood in silence as Marie finished her story— deep, deep sadness penetrating every inch of our beings.

Burt prayed for Marie and we left her resting alone in the care of the U.S. army medics of the 8th field hospital.

I was sick, angry, drained. Bob Ziemer was the tribes field chairman who had met EG and me at the Saigon airport when we had first arrived. Bob had dedicated each of our children to God at Dalat conferences. He was also the translator of the Raday New Testament and the teacher of our Jarai pastors at the Banmethuout Bible School.

Marie was the one who accompanied me when I sang. Our lives had been intertwined during my many trips to the Leprosarium.

I suddenly felt older. It wasn't a great leap to imagine EG in Marie's place and me dead!

Back in 1960 our cook had drawn my attention to a certain bird call.

"Listen, Ong," he had said. "That is very bad. That bird's call is 'Cac quan bo cuc (all soldiers gather for extreme hardship).' That means there will be a great war with many killed."

Many times I would remember that prediction but I didn't know it would come to this.

On our way back to the Sutherlands' we stopped at the Christian Service Men's Center and discovered a house full of evacuated missionaries. Dave Frazier's smiling face greeted us as he opened the tall gate to the property. What a relief it was to see him and the rest of the Pleiku contingent safe and sound. They, too, had a story to tell.

When the communists arrived in Pleiku, they overran the southwestern quadrant of the city. Our house marked the border between the southwestern and the southeastern quadrant. The heaviest fighting in the city began within 150 feet of our back yard and ran for about a mile through to the southwest.

Despite the proximity of our house to the fighting, its fortress-like walls afforded the best protection against stray gunfire. So the five remaining missionaries—David and Jeannie Frazier, Keith Kayser, Dawn Deets and Joan (Waller) Downs, plus the Fraziers' three small children—hid there. For 10 hours they lay flat on the floor, not daring to move even as the skirmishes came as close as our yard.

At one point early in the fighting David opened the front door a crack to look out. He found himself on the business end of an M-79 grenade launcher toted by an ARVN soldier. Dave did a brave and very wise thing—he swung the door open and showed his face so the gunner would know there were Americans in the house. That act may have spared all their lives.

By Tuesday noon the fighting had subsided sufficiently for all of them to get to the air base. From there, two days later, they got a flight to Nhatrang.

Dave was surprised to see me at the Christian Service Men's Center. They had heard a rumor that a pilot had seen a Caucasian woman and two blond-headed little girls out in the forest northwest of Nhatrang. They thought it might be EG and our girls. I was thankful it wasn't true.

Dave also had a little joke for me. During more serene days in Pleiku an American sergeant had come across a 40-pound box of frozen steaks that was more than their freezers could handle, so he gave it to me. I had placed it in our freezer. When the Fraziers evacuated they had brought the steaks with them. The Nhatrang market was closed all week, so the "poor" missionaries had eaten my steaks. They all thanked me for my contribution to their evacuation!

We proceeded back to the Sutherlands' under the same conditions—no other cars on the road, no other people moving about. The Viet Cong were trapped in the city and trying to escape. Occasional gunfire could be heard.

Monday, February 5, Dave and I decided to try to get back to Pleiku to close up our houses. When we arrived at the Nhatrang airport the French consul was negotiating with Air America to evacuate the

French tourists whom we had met on the plane from Saigon. When the tourists saw me they all started chattering at once with hands flailing the air.

It seemed they had been on the beach Tuesday morning unaware of the battle. VC came running toward them, pursued by Korean troops. The French hit the sand as the VC ran over them, followed by the Koreans. Those were some excited tourists!

Dave and I managed to hitch a ride on an Air America single-engined aircraft built for short take-offs and landings. We climbed on board.

The flight, they told us, was to stop in Banmethuot. That was an unexpected turn of events. The trip was uneventful until we began our descent. Suddenly we heard groundfire. The pilot pulled the plane up and circled briefly. From our vantage point we could see that the mission station and a huge community of houses around it had burned in the fighting.

On the second attempt to land, the pilot literally spiraled the plane onto the runway. We were happy to finally be on terra firma. From what we could see from the windows of the plane, everyone on the ground seemed to be at war. There was shooting everywhere. We let off some passengers, then took off, banking sharply and spiraling up within the base's barbed wire perimeter.

✦   ✦   ✦

In actuality, Tet 1968 was a signal victory for the Allies. Few ever really appreciated that. During all the preceding years, there had been large numbers of "closet" communists throughout South Vietnam. During the Tet offensive these locals were so sure of instant victory that they stepped out into the streets with their guns blazing. And when they started shooting, the army killed them—the American army, the Vietnamese army, the Korean army.

The communists lost thousands of people in the Tet offensive. Most of them were local Viet Cong. After that, VC activity dropped like a spent rocket. And from then on, the war was strictly outside intervention from the North.

But the Tet offensive galvanized the United States' attitude against an already unpopular war. What was, in fact, a stunning defeat for North Vietnam ironically marked the beginning of North Vietnam's triumph.

For The Christian and Missionary Alliance, Tet 1968 resulted in the largest single loss of missionaries since the 1910 Boxer Rebellion in China. Once more, as in 1962, the highland town of Banmethuot was the focal point.

Five missionaries—Ed and Ruth Thompson, Carolyn Griswold, Ruth Wilting, Robert Ziemer—plus Carolyn's visiting father, Leon Griswold, died as the Viet Cong overran the Mission property on the outskirts of town. Another Leprosarium worker, Betty Olsen, as well as Wycliffe missionary, Henry Blood, and a civilian forestry expert, Mike Benge, were taken captive.

Betty Olsen and Henry Blood died in the jungle. Mike Benge was eventually released and returned to the States.

17

Magnificent Obsession

Dave and I arrived at Pleiku in the afternoon. The base was humming. The A1 Skyraiders were being hustled in and out for ammunition. Choppers were all around, as if they were searching for something.

"What are you looking for, Colonel?" I asked as we came on the base commander.

"VC!" he responded curtly.

"Right now, in broad daylight? This close?"

"Yes, sir," he responded. "They have been everywhere."

Welcome back to Pleiku, I thought. *Stay alert, keep moving and give no one a shot at you.*

We hitched a ride into town. Buildings on every side were bullet-riddled. The government offices were pockmarked. Burned-out vehicles obstructed the streets.

We went directly to the Mission compound. Only the Jarai yardman was there.

Tree limbs lay where bullets had trimmed them from the pines. Dave went to his house and I went to mine, to pack up our stuff and secure the property until the situation improved. Pastor Phong warned us in no uncertain terms to leave before sunset and to not return until well into the morning.

We took his advice and about 4 p.m. we headed for the 71st Medivac Hospital where Dave and the Pleiku missionaries had spent several days before being evacuated to Nhatrang. Our nurses and the Mennonite nurses had helped the hospital staff because of the large number of casualties during the heat of the battle. Special Forces Captain Larry Dring had three inches of femoral artery shot out of his right leg. Dave and I bade him farewell as he was moved to the airfield for a flight to Tokyo.

I took two G.I. mattresses and slept between them, making a Charlie sandwich on the floor of a large empty ward. The lights were on all night. I toyed with shrapnel stuck in the wall above my head from the last rocket attack.

The next day Dave and I returned to the compound to finish the packing. Pastor Phong and his family helped us, probably at great risk. What a precious, Christ-like man! I loved that man. He had been the driving force as we preached at a local prison every Saturday afternoon over a two-year period—he in Vietnamese, I in Jarai. Out of about 750 prisoners, 350 had become Christians.

During that time Pastor Phong caught bubonic plague, which I suspect came from the prison. After he had passed the delirium stage I often sat at his bedside. He would clasp my hands with his two hands.

"It is really true," he would say weakly, "that even

though we are different races and languages we are one in Jesus Christ." EG and I had given him three injections of streptomycin per day until he recovered.

Now he and his family stuck with me until we packed our most precious things in 55-gallon steel drums, sold other things and gave away some.

That day we worked with the shutters closed. There was sporadic fighting on the hill across the creek. Bullets whizzed through the yard. VC were hidden in kitchens, wells, etc. When they were discovered, a gunfight or grenade fight would ensue. I kept my 12-gauge shotgun loaded and laid out across the top of a drum wherever we worked. I was determined not to be gunned down at this point. I would defend myself.

I let it be known that I wanted to sell a lot of stuff. Rev. Sang bought my blue VW truck. I had installed a seatbelt in it. It had oversized tires and a glass fuel bowl so I could see water in the line. I didn't want to part with it. What had been worth $15,000 before Tet was now worth $2,000!

An American soldier bought my big black TWN motorcycle. A Jarai bought our beautiful mahogany bed. Even at bargain prices people weren't buying much.

We left the houses so that someone else could move in if they came before we finished our furloughs. All of our belongings were stored in the garage. Though I knew that what I was doing was the wise choice, I hated the thought of leaving so many great and sentimental memories and an unfinished dream—the translation.

I wanted in the worst way to stay in Pleiku. In just four years the Jarai Christians had increased to over 2,000. Even the provincial chief and his wife were believers.

The new leprosy treatment center in Pleiku was almost ready for us. Most of the funding for its construction had come from American GIs interested in our work. Its inauguration could not come too soon. We were by then treating 1,500 patients a month. I was especially grateful for the team of Vietnamese and Jarai caregivers who were still faithfully at work.

But Pleiku was a war zone. Under such conditions our activities would be limited and our personal danger magnified. To stay would be foolhardy.

There was one item of value that I could neither pack nor even retrieve: the rough manuscript of Matthew's Gospel. It was my first serious translation attempt and for that reason was very important. I had worked on it over in the school which stood some 50 yards from our house in an exposed area of the compound. I considered going over to get it, but the shutterless windows offered no protection from the lurking enemy.

I decided that I would just have to let Matthew wait until a later trip. It was a hard decision to make. Perhaps I would never be able to retrieve it. I didn't know.

Dave and I returned to Nhatrang only to find that our instructions were to proceed to Cam Ranh Bay Naval Base. Suddenly a lot of families were occupying a tent city that had been made for male troops. EG and I were lucky—we had a large squad tent to ourselves. Three times a day buses transported us to a distant mess hall for meals. Two of our missionary men were placed in charge of all Alliance evacuees on the base.

Our orders from the Vietnamese government and our Mission in Saigon were that none of us was to leave the country without an exit visa. Messengers from Saigon talked to us about staying in Vietnam and preparing to go back to our stations. I had just gone through the experience of not acting forcefully enough to save the lives of the Banmethuot missionaries. I found the idea of returning to our stations incomprehensible.

"The current situation is not going to improve for many months," I began as I stood to my feet. "The whole plateau is a battleground. American soldiers just risked their lives to save yours. It is unfair to expect them to do that again. Anyone who goes back now will be responsible for his life and his family's lives and maybe some young soldier's life. I am not going back until things have settled down."

Most of the missionaries decided to go to safe havens to wait out the Tet aftermath. It would be nine months before anyone could live safely on the Pleiku station.

I went to visit Marie at Cam Ranh hospital. Her daughter, Beth, and son-in-law, Rick Drummond, were with her. They were in a quandary. Within a few minutes the Air Force was planning to evacuate Marie to the U.S. There was room on the C-141 for the Drummonds to accompany her.

"What should we do?" Rick asked. "Orders are

not to leave without exit visas. Bob and Dale are in charge but there's no time to contact them."

Obviously Marie needed her daughter desperately. We could not behave ourselves as if we were robots without any sense of feeling or loss. Marie was terribly wounded. She was also going home to bury Bob. Besides, she had no home of her own in the States.

"You guys go home with her," I said. "Love her. Protect her. Help her. Bless her. Don't sweat the visas. If Vietnam won't let you return after these circumstances, it doesn't deserve your presence. I'll take personal responsibility to the Mission for your leaving. You take care of your mother!"

✦ ✦ ✦

My parents received a telegram from our New York Mission office on February 20: "Your son Charles and family in Tanah Rata, Malaysia. Left Saigon February 16. Cowles, Foreign Dept."

EG and I were within four months of our normal furlough. Under the circumstances we could have elected to go home early but Dalat School, by then in Malaysia, was in urgent need of dorm parents for the high school boys. We agreed to take on that responsibility for the spring semester.

Meanwhile in Vietnam the contractor continued to build the Leprosy Center. I was invited to attend the dedication.

I accompanied the Vietnam MKs returning to Saigon. From my window seat I watched as the Air Vietnam Boeing 727 descended to about 1,000 feet and lined up with the Saigon runway.

Suddenly, off the left wing, I saw a large orange explosion about a kilometer away and watched as a Skyraider (dive bomber) nosed up, leaving the scene. Choppers moved in and were firing in the same area.

Our pilot flinched! He, like the rest of us, had heard and felt the blast. He gave full power, aborted the landing and went around for a second attempt.

I thought, *What am I coming back to? If this fighting is in Saigon, what is happening elsewhere?*

That night four mortar rounds exploded within a block or two of The Christian and Missionary Alliance guest home. They were loud! They were very businesslike! I slept the last hours of the night on the tile floor beneath the mattress. Just a little terrorism to let you know the enemy is there! Whoever is in the way, however, gets hurt!

Morning dawned, quiet and peaceful.

The next day I went to the airport with our field chairman, Franklin Irwin. Franklin and I knew each other well. He had worked with the Vietnamese resettlement villages of Pleiku and visited us many times.

The aging DC-4 seemed worn out. They must have had to repair something because we were three hours late. My attitude was, *if Air Vietnam wants to fix something it must be broke bad! I can wait!*

The plane finally creaked out onto the runway and took its place in the morning lineup. Tan Son Nhut airport had become the busiest airport in the world during the war. From my vantage point in

the back I could see oil streaming over the left in-
board engine's cowling. I thanked the Lord that I
was in His hand and not that of the delapidated
plane.

Praise the Lord, the flight was uneventful. We
bounced steadily down through low, early-rainy-
season clouds and touched the black asphalt runway of the military base known as New Pleiku. Safe
again! We were rushed to the dedication 11
kilometers from town.

Under a large cargo-parachute tent, chairs had
been arranged in a semi-circle. The Pleiku Vietnamese church and choir were there. It was
wonderful to see so many old friends, including
some American troops. A Huie helicopter arrived,
carrying the highest ranking dignitary, General
Peers, commander of the Fourth Infantry Division.

It was a dream come true—the leprosy hospital
was actually finished! But Ruth Wilting, who had
contributed so much to our leprosy work in Pleiku
province, had died at Banmethout in February. It
was a bittersweet day.

Olive Kingsbury was there, too. It was her car
that the VC had used to abduct the three missionaries at the Leprosarium in 1962. She missed
the Banmethout Tet massacre because she was in
Nhatrang visiting the doctor.

The Leprosy Center dedication was the good
news of the day. The bad news was the happenings
at the Pleiku station the night before.

The Bible school building had been bombed!
Dawn Deets, Joan Downs and Olive Kingsbury, we
were told, had been asleep in their nearby house;

Keith Keyser in his about 50 yards away. We went to take a look.

To protect the Bible school building from vandals, tribesmen slept in a front room each night. One of the men greeted us at the gate.

"Oh, how happy to see you!" he said quietly. "I am so sorry for what has happened here. I should have defended it better. I was asleep. I heard the glass break in Mr. Long's office, then the wall fell on me and the fierce heat and smoke came in. My head was hurt and bleeding. The VC sappers crept close and put the bomb through the window."

I entered the building. The brick and mortar interior wall lay beside the watchman's sleeping mat. Dave's large metal cabinet had diverted the wall from falling directly on him. The ceiling and roof were blown away, leaving open sky above.

I stepped over the shattered wall into my office. My desk was unrecognizable kindling wood. Already many people had trampled through, just looking. Papers, lessons, supplies were strewn across the floor. The spines of all the books on the shelves looked alike—burned black.

The whole exterior wall was blown out and the explosion had blasted a hole in the cement floor right down to red earth.

I shuffled through the rubble, kicking it back and forth with my foot. I had only one prized possession in mind—the translated portions of the Bible.

And then I spied it! On the floor, torn and trampled, was the notebook containing my Matthew translation. Miracle of miracles, the pages inside were still intact and legible. I vowed I would never again let any of the translation work out of my sight.

But there was more news to come! All the other missionaries were clearing out, leaving me on the station by myself for the night.

As darkness fell a jeep arrived at the compound. A chaplain's driver brought me the "wonderful" news that intelligence had heard that there were 150 VC in town to blow up American buildings during the night. That was precisely how the Bible school building had been blown up the previous night!

I was to stay in the single ladies' house. It was the third building inside the front gate after the Bible school and the old tin-sided clinic. I would be sleeping about 50 yards from the last explosion!

Darkness fell about 6 p.m. It was a rainy night with heavy cloud cover. I thought, *What am I doing here? I have plane tickets for a trip home! Somehow I have to survive tonight!*

The bedroom was in the middle of the house on the front side. The front wall had a window. I kept the door shut to stop any light from showing out the back side of the building which was the direction where, about 50 feet away, the slaughter of the Tet offensive had taken place.

"Now I lay me down to sleep; I pray the Lord my soul to keep. If I should die before I wake, I pray Thee, Lord, my soul to take." I read the Bible, then turned off the light and lay down in the single bed with my head to the front wall by the window. I closed my eyes but my brain was racing, reexamining the whole station.

Where should I go that is safer than this? All the other

buildings are locked. I can't get into them. Just go out and hide among the trees! The mosquitos and black ants will give you a great night! Shut up and get to sleep! Tomorrow will be here soon.

I could hear the grass growing. Ants made loud crawling sounds in the yard. *Go to sleep!* I couldn't. I turned the lamp on again.

A Louis L'Amour book lay near the bed. I started to read, my ears ever trained on the night sounds. About 11 p.m. chopper engines began to roar at Camp Holloway and head my way, their steady buzz honing in on the station. Then came the pop of their blades and the Doppler high to low sounds as they rotored west. I heard the pop of flares igniting high overhead.

I turned off the light and watched the flarelight make eerie shadows of the many trees of the Pleiku station. A chopper zoomed west and rockets were fired at who knows what about two miles away.

The choppers finally returned to base and it was quiet, except for the fire of U.S. and Vietnamese *H and I* (harassment and interdiction) artillery. *H and I* means random rounds fired at trails, crossroads or suspected VC gathering points. The shooting went on all night.

About one o'clock I felt sleepy. I turned off the light and snuggled the pillow. Boom! A grenade or boobytrap exploded. I prayed for all the Jarai names I could remember, gunfire both near and distant ringing in my ears.

Then the big drum, cymbals and bells sounded their slow, never-ending rhythm from the Buddhist pagoda on the east border of the compound. I prayed for the work of the gospel in Pleiku and throughout Vietnam. I prayed for the U.S. troops and their safety. I did not sleep the whole night.

The next day I worked around the compound and in the late afternoon headed for the air base where a chaplain had arranged sleeping quarters for me. I was given a top bunk in the doctor's quarters, a room surrounded by a three-foot wall of sandbags.

About 1 a.m. 122-millimeter rockets began to crunch in. "Incoming!" a voice in the darkness yelled. I grabbed the flack jacket and helmet off the wall and slipped into them as I leaped off the bunk. The doctor below me had just moved to hit the deck, too. I flattened him. We lay there laughing.

I began counting rockets—all 25 of them. They hit short, out near the barbed wire but also in a nearby Jarai village. Four houses were destroyed, one person killed and more wounded.

The next day I finished my work, ate with a few close Vietnamese friends that night and departed the next morning. I can't find words to decribe the feelings, but my jaw was clenched tight.

✦ ✦ ✦

We began our second furlough as scheduled in July, 1968. God provided a brand-new furnished three-bedroom apartment near a Christian school in Charlotte. The manager was a Christian and leased us the showpiece model apartment of a large complex. All we needed were linens and kitchenware.

I wanted to treat EG like a queen. She had been through four years of dirt, inconvenience, terror, hard work and sick children. I so wanted to bless her with a place of peace, comfort, convenience and retreat.

Within days I was off to speak at Mahaffey Camp in western Pennsylvania. I had toughed it out in Vietnam for four years. Like a battle-hardened soldier, I had never let my guard down.

One night, with over 2,000 people in the audience, I told the story of the deaths of our missionaries at Banmethuout. Then, in their memory, I sang, "O Love That Wilt Not Let Me Go." The last two lines came up from the depths of my soul: "I lay in dust, life's glory dead/ And from the ground there blossoms red/ Life that shall endless be."

I turned from the sea of faces and returned to my seat. As I sat down, years of pent-up grief and sorrow poured out of me. With my head in both hands I wept uncontrollably, deep sobs heaving my chest, tears staining the unfinished boards of the platform. I had no handkerchief and no one offered me one. All alone, before a large crowd, God washed away my sorrows.

That fall my missionary tour assignment was in Ohio. I was anxious to get home, so after the last service, I packed up the new Ford LTD that had been loaned to me by my brother-in-law and headed south. It was already 9 p.m.

Close friends had been ruthlessly killed in an endless war. Death was easy to come by. Our precious children were ten, eight, four and two years of age.

Christian friends asked, "Are you really going to take your children back over there?" It seemed that the price of loving Vietnam had become steeper.

As I drove through the freezing cold in the comfort of the car, I began to mull over the decision we would have to make. The West Virginia Turnpike was deep in slush, with about 14 inches of snow glistening in the moonlight on the slopes. There was nothing like that in Vietnam!

The roads were clear and dry as I pulled up at a gas station some time later. Ready to go again, I lowered the electric seat, cinched the seatbelt tight and prepared for the last several hours to Charlotte.

How could I risk the lives of EG and the children again?

The road curved and tilted slowly left along the top of a ridge. An 18-wheeler was coming toward me. I could see that at the top of the ridge snow had blown across my lane. I braked, then when I hit the snow I released the brake, trying to hold the car straight and steady.

It shot off the snow and onto the dry pavement—right at the truck. I braked again, still heading straight for the headlights of the approaching truck. At the last second I turned back into my lane and onto the packed snow. The car skidded to the right and began to fall back off the snow into the truck's lane. His tail lights flashed by. Whew!

The car then turned down the hill, propelled by the weight of the engine. The right front of the car smashed through the snow piles left by the plow, and suddenly there was no road noise. I was airborne! The car landed on its top and rolled several times, finally ending up on its roof.

Suspended upside down by the seatbelt, I turned off the lights and the ignition and listened for fire. I heard none. I loosened the seat belt and tried to get out. The snow was deep. The hardtop was bent. I couldn't get the door open, nor could I reach my coat in the back seat.

I began to turn the headlights on and off in an effort to attract someone. There was little traffic. At last, as I shivered in the 20-degree cold, two truck drivers stopped. I heard one say, "Nobody could be alive in there!" The other replied, "He must be. He's turning the headlights on and off!"

I yelled for them to come and get me. Within minutes they had slid the 50 or so feet down the ravine and managed to dig me out. I was unhurt, even though my head and shoulders had left a bulge on an otherwise flattened roof. The car was declared "totaled."

"Charlie," the Lord said, "You could die in North Carolina or Virginia as easily as in Vietnam. You had better obey me!"

I responded in true military fashion: "Aye, aye, Sir!"

✦ ✦ ✦

We were still at home in March, 1969 when Richard Nixon's Secretary of Defense, Melvin Laird, announced the "Vietnamization" of the Indo-China war. The United States began to shift more and more of the combat fighting onto the

South Vietnamese. By the time we returned to Vietnam that summer, the first units of American troops were being withdrawn.

As we began our third term, it would have been easy to make Dalat School our full-time work. The need for houseparents seemed perennial. But EG and I had been sent as missionaries to Vietnam. We had learned the Vietnamese language. We had learned the Jarai language.

And, probably most important, we were concerned because the Jarai people did not have an adequate translation of the Scriptures in their tongue. My call to missions had centered around the translation of the Scriptures. By this point it was an obsession! I knew I might not yet be an expert in Jarai, but I considered myself proficient. Besides, no one else was in a position to spearhead such a task.

The next two years were spent working four months at the school, then two months in Vietnam, on a rotating basis.

Few of us expected South Vietnam to survive for long. The government was being propped up by outside powers, notably the United States. The question was not *if* South Vietnam would fall, but *when*. If the Jarai were to have the Scriptures in their own language it was now or never.

I grew a beard, vowing I would not shave until the Jarai New Testament was finished. But even as I set myself to the lengthy, painstaking task, the third part of this love story moved into a new and glorious dimension.

The first part—the deep love that EG and I

shared—was alive and well.

The second part—God's love for me and my commitment to Him and my desire to obey Him—likewise held firm.

Now, the great and generous God who loved the world enough to give His only Son to be its Savior began a new, powerful and widespread demonstration of His love for the Montagnards of South Vietnam. It began far from the tribal villages of the highlands.

The withdrawal of American combat troops meant, in practical terms, that the Vietnamese were taking more serious casualties than ever. To replace these casualties, the government was conscripting every possible recruit for military duty. That, in turn, offered a remarkable opportunity to evangelize, for the South Vietnamese government had long been open to Christian ministry among its armed forces.

The Mission rule was that any new ministry had to be approved by the executive committee before it was initiated. There was one notorious breaker of that rule—Ruth Jeffries, daughter of the famed Jonathan Goforth, missionary to China. She had a way of starting big and successful projects, then going in tears to the committee to plead for personnel and funds to continue it.

Such was the case with Ruth's popular *Dawn* magazine, an evangelistic publication sold nationwide in secular bookstores.

In much the same way she began her ministry to the military at the main Vietnamese Army Induction Center and at the large Cong Hoa (Kaam

WHA) Military Hospital. When she appealed to the executive committee for help, what could they say but yes?

So the field conference responded by assigning several Saigon missionary couples to this work— Garth and Betty Hunt, Jim and Jean Livingston, David and Linda Hartzfeld and a newly-arrived missionary couple, Phil and Sandy Young.

They all lived on one compound and worked at the induction center and military hospital, giving each recruit a Gospel of John and ministering spiritually to those who returned wounded.

God gave great success to their work. Many soldiers turned to Christ through their witness, but it was emotionally exhausting work. As the ministry stretched into 1969, 1970 and the beginning of 1971 without respite, the team of missionaries was finally becoming burned out.

Garth Hunt assessed the problem: "Men were dying and they needed Christ. Any personal sacrifices were justified, I felt, 'to reach a nation for God.' [But] I foolishly sacrificed what I needed most—spiritual well-being, physical health and my family. Nothing had been withheld, the task came first, the crisis must be met."

Garth sensed a growing conviction that his only hope for spiritual renewal and rehabilitation was a fresh baptism of the Holy Spirit. He decided to extricate himself from some of his involvement in the ministry and set aside time to wait on the Lord.

One by one the other missionary couples on the compound also joined in the quest. Week after week they prayed. And God poured His living water into their thirsty souls.

"God met our hearts with a stupendous and awesome joy of His presence during those days," remembers Jim Livingston. "He flooded our souls with a holy brokenness. He bathed our lives with a flood of love and peace and hope, right in the midst of Vietnam's most shattering years."

But that was only the beginning. The repercussions of those days could hardly be imagined.

18

Visit From God

The year 1971 marked the 60th anniversary of Alliance missionary work in Vietnam. In keeping with the significance of this event, the Church and Mission invited Billy Graham to speak at the Annual National Church Conference, to be held at the International Protestant Church in Saigon.

Dr. Graham sent his regrets.

The Church and Mission then invited an outstanding Alliance pastor, Rev. William E. Allen, a man of missions, church growth and deep spiritual life. Pastor Allen and his Mansfield, Ohio church had been fired by the Canadian revival of 1970. He agreed to address not only the National Church Conference but the Missionary Field Conference immediately following.

The International Protestant Church in Saigon was a long, rectangular building with a sanctuary that could seat as many as 1,000. The front of the sanctuary was made of pink marble terrazzo with a high concrete platform. Rows of windows on either side had long since been taped to reduce their vulnerability and danger in a country at war. Nevertheless, the sanctuary afforded a bright and spacious setting for the preaching of the Word by Pastor Allen.

"I'll never forget that first service," he commented later. "The building was jammed with people and the faces outside looked to be 50 deep. As I sat there waiting to speak I could not keep back the tears. I thought of Robert Ziemer and the other Banmethuot martyrs and the tremendous price they and many others had paid to make this scene possible. At the time we had about 100,000 believers in Vietnam. Without the tremendous work of our missionaries this could not possibly have happened."

God moved in a remarkable way during that week as Rev. Allen preached twice each day to capacity crowds of Vietnamese. On one occasion at least, the service lasted four hours, including the message, the interpretation by Tom Stebbins and prayer and anointing for the many who pressed forward for healing.

The Saturday evening before the Missionary Conference was to begin, a number of missionaries gathered at the Gia Dinh compound for a time of prayer. God broke in, visiting them with a great refreshing and filling their hearts to overflowing.

The next day we convened at the church to begin our conference. After the thousands of Vietnamese who had packed out the building the preceding week, 75 missionaries looked like a mere handful. Normally we would have met at Dalat, but by 1971 Dalat was too dangerous for such a gathering. So we sacrificed the invigorating air of the highlands in favor of sultry Saigon.

God proved to be no respecter of numbers. As Pastor Allen began to speak to us, conviction fell. Not everyone was touched at the same moment. It was as if the Holy Spirit was working individually, in turn, person by person.

As He did His personal work, each one would stand and confess his or her sins openly. Other missionaries would then lovingly gather around them to pray and to give encouragement.

One particuarly touching scene involved Beth Drummond. Beth was a second-generation missionary, the daughter of Robert and Marie Ziemer. Just three years earlier her father had been martyred in the Tet offensive. Beth stood and testified that ever since her teens she had been terrorized by thoughts of Satan and his power.

"Perhaps," she said, "it had something to do with my growing up in a land where evil spirits were worshiped and greatly feared." Beth was afraid of the dark. She always slept with the light on when her husband, Rick, was not home.

Beth and Rick lived on the outskirts of Quang Ngai. The Viet Cong had a habit of running through the Drummonds' front yard on their way into town to fight. This, of course, didn't help Beth's peace of mind. After the skirmish, the communists would run through the yard again, with South Vietnamese soldiers in hot pursuit. While all of this was going on, the Drummonds would be flat on the floor in their bedroom.

All of us in Vietnam knew fear. It was the way of life in Vietnam during those years. But I for one had never thought about fear as a sin. "The Lord Jesus showed me very clearly," Beth said, "that He had triumphed over Satan on Calvary. Since I belonged to Jesus, I did not have to fear Satan at all!"

The triumphant One, to whom Beth belonged, released her first from her abnormal fear of Satan and then from fear for the physical safety of her family.

As we listened to Beth we were all acutely aware that God was in that sanctuary. The entire session was a time of literal melting before God. Any kind of hardness did not have a place in the sanctuary of the International Protestant Church in Saigon that day.

Early in the meeting the Lord got hold of me, too. I realized that my prayer life had been stilted and formal. I would get down on my knees to pray but I was inclined to be lazy and dull. Prayer time for me was almost like a rest period.

As the Holy Spirit began pressing in upon me, I got up in the middle of the meeting and began pacing back and forth at the back of the sanctuary, praying. I found that I did not get sleepy while I was walking. I experienced such an overwhelming spirit of prayer as I talked to God very personally about everything. Walking and praying became a habit for me.

I also remember Bob McNeel. Bob had not been well. A peptic ulcer, said the doctors. Bob had already made flight reservations for a medical furlough in the States. But Bob walked down to the front pew of the church and sat down. As the fellows gathered around he said quite simply, "Pray for me. I want to be healed. I don't want to go home."

We were Bob's buddies, close friends. All of us had been through it. We had been shot at. We had risked our lives for the gospel. Though still living we were already dead men. We had already passed beyond some barriers in this life.

So we started to pray for Bob. As we did so a spirit of hilarity came upon us all and we began to laugh. You would have thought we were irreverent, but we couldn't help it. We stood around Bob, laughing and praying at the same time that God would heal him.

Bob started laughing, too, and crying out to the Lord. When he got home to the States, doctors could find no ulcer! God had performed a miracle.

Eleven years of intensive use of Jarai had prepared me linguistically for my work of translating the New Testament and Psalms into Jarai. But now, by the gracious infusion of Himself, God was equipping me spiritually for the task. Little could I envision, as we basked in the radiance of God's presence there in our Saigon conference, how His special presence would impact my ministry.

Neither could any of us guess what a remarkable work of sovereign grace God was poised to do throughout all of South Vietnam, but especially in the highlands among the Montagnard tribespeople.

19

The Revival Spreads

T he missionary conference in Saigon was an exhilarating week—to put it mildly. In addition to the business sessions and the preaching, there were impromptu nights of prayer and confession and testimony. We aired our misunderstandings. We found new joy and power. Many of us were freshly filled with the Holy Spirit.

For the five missionary families in the Nhatrang area especially, a new atmosphere of love and joy prevailed. Their regular Tuesday evening prayer meeting was not enough. They began meeting more frequently to share their spiritual victories and to pray for each other. God had touched their hearts and they longed to see the revival spread to the Vietnamese church.

That fall, Orrel Steinkamp, a professor at the Tin Lanh National Church Seminary at Nhatrang, experienced the blessing of the Saigon revival. Back at the seminary, he received permission to add a new course to the school's curriculum: *History of Revivals.* After several weeks of discussing the Scriptural basis for revival, Orrel assigned students to research and to report on specific major revivals.

Each report seemed to whet the hunger of the students. A group of them began to meet at five o'clock each morning to pray for revival at Nhatrang.

On Friday, December 3, a student was scheduled to report on the recent revival in Indonesia. Another class also came to Room 5 to hear the report. As it turned out, almost half of the school's 117 students were present to witness the beginning of revival at Nhatrang that would sweep the tribal districts of South Vietnam—a revival that continues to this day.

At the conclusion of the report, the students appealed for prayer for revival in Vietnam to begin right there at the seminary. They bowed their heads and first one, then another, led in prayer. At first the praying was not unusual. But then one of the students began to weep and to confess specific sins.

Suddenly, as Orrel Steinkamp put it, "the room was alive with spontaneous, simultaneous prayer." God's Spirit fell upon that group of students.

When the rest of the student body showed up for lunch at the empty dining room, many of them made their way to Room 5 and were soon caught up in what was happening. Students sought out each other to confess hatred, cheating, stealing. Some repented of jealousy. It was common to see three or four students locked in a weeping embrace.

The students also began coming to Orrel and other missionaries, asking them to pray that they would be filled with the Holy Spirit. As those prayers were answered the students burst out with hallelujahs and spontaneous songs of praise. It was a scene repeated over and over that day.

With only brief intermissions for meals, the gathering lasted until 2:30 in the morning. It was a full week before the seminary got back to some semblance of its regular schedule.

The pattern was conviction—deep, awful conviction of sin—followed by confession and then tremendous comfort as God brought cleansing. Then exhilarating praise and finally, witness to others. And that same pattern prevailed wherever the revival spread: conviction, confession, cleansing, comfort, praise and witness.

✦ ✦ ✦

At the school that year there were five Koho (Kaa HAW) students (*Koho* means "barbarian"). Seven distinct tribes make up the Koho peoples. Their dialects are similar enough that they can understand each other.

Two of these five Koho boys were not on speaking terms and a third was so desperately ill with recurring stomach problems that he was on the verge of leaving school.

During the revival the two young men who were not speaking to each other got right with God and with each other. Tam (TAAM), the sick one, requested prayer not only to be filled with the Spirit but also to be healed.

"We prayed for the fullness of the Spirit," Orrel said, "then I simply placed my hand on his stomach. 'In Jesus' name,' I said, 'we claim healing for this man.' "

"And he was healed! In fact, the next morning, he testified that instead of the usual bland rice water he normally drank, he could now eat anything— even hot red peppers!"

Word of what had happened at Nhatrang was not long in reaching the highland city of Dalat. Helen Evans, for one, was looking forward to the Christmas recess and the homecoming of the five Koho students.

"God gave us a Christmas never to be forgotten!" Helen reported. "I had the privilege of being present on December 22 when the Lord came down on the young people in Dalat. They presented their long-practiced Christmas program and were relaxing with soda and cookies.

"It was about 11:30 p.m. when two of the Nhatrang students began to tell us how God had worked in their hearts. They urged their friends to confess every sin to the Lord and receive His forgiveness; then the Holy Spirit would fill them.

"At first, just a few started to pray quietly. Then one teenager began to sob as he told the Lord how he had deceived his parents and done other sinful things. I heard someone singing, 'Just as I am, without one plea . . .' as he slowly made his way to the front of the church.

"Soon everyone was praying aloud, doing business with God," Helen continued. "Brokenhearted teenagers flung themselves at my knees, sobbing out their sins to the Lord, asking my forgiveness for certain things and wanting me to pray with them.

As various ones got everything right with God and with each other, the Holy Spirit filled them. . . .

"The following day most of them went to their villages for Christmas. As they told what had happened to them, the Lord began to convict of sin. Adults, teenagers and children confessed sin and experienced God's forgiveness. In a new surge of faith the young people led the way in praying for those who were sick or physically afflicted. Countless ones were healed, demons were cast out . . . ."

Wherever the five Koho students went, God's presence accompanied them. Weak and cold Christians confessed their sins and were revived. One pastor was instantly healed. All his children repented of their sins.

And Koho believers gave 500,000 piasters (approximately $2,000) in withheld tithes!

20

Fired-Up Jarai

A few months later the National Tribal Conference was held at Dalat. Once again the Lord met the assembly in an unusual way. And the fires of revival, so brightly burning at Dalat, were carried by the delegates to their home churches.

When the Pleiku delegates returned home, they brought the revival with them. The Jarai called it "the heightened revelation of spiritual power." They already knew God. But now He was there in a much different role, staging a great demonstration of power and revival, cleansing sin-stained lives. And people prayed and were filled with the Holy Spirit.

Over the next three years I tabulated 23,000 new believers in nine highland tribes. One tribe alone had 10,000 new believers.

In one village a sorcerer received Christ. He then prayed to be filled with the Holy Spirit. Instantly, demons attacked him and knocked him down. Other Christians prayed for him and the demons departed. He was restored and filled with the Spirit.

In Pleiku a man prayed to be filled with the Holy Spirit. Demons attacked him and a few others. Christians prayed and all were delivered.

All the while, people were being healed and a young pastor described preaching as "easy work" as his listeners had freedom to respond. New churches sprang up everywhere, even in places where just weeks before there had been no believers.

One of the Pleiku deacons preached regularly in a village where we had a leprosy center. A blind man, attracted by the singing, listened for several weeks to the gospel. Then, unknown to the deacon, he had a vision of heaven.

The next time the deacon preached, his subject was heaven. The blind man interrupted.

"I have *seen* heaven," he said after hearing what heaven was like. He then prayed to receive Christ as his Savior.

In the Pleiku hospital Vietnamese received Christ as our Jarai pastors witnessed. It is unusual for a tribal preacher to lead a Vietnamese, one of the majority people, to Christ. But this was common in the Pleiku area during the revival. Even after South Vietnam fell to the communists, Vietnamese soldiers who had heard the gospel from Jarai ministers sought them out and wanted to receive Christ.

A Jarai major in the Vietnamese army commanded an artillery post south of Pleiku. In a night attack in the fall of 1972, communists overran the post, taking this officer as a prisoner. He was held in a Viet Cong camp deep in the jungle.

By day he and his fellow prisoners were forced to dig and plant gardens. At night they were kept in a small bamboo stockade.

In the stockade the prisoners, hands tied behind them, were locked in waist-high bamboo stocks. Then their ankles were tied to another length of bamboo high enough from the ground so that their feet were suspended. Each night was spent in this very painful position, with all the body weight resting on wrists and ankles.

One night the major had a dream. In his dream he was walking down the road carrying a pole with a cross on the top of it. On each side of the road there were people yelling, "Welcome!" as though they were welcoming him home.

When he awoke, he was puzzled. He had heard the gospel and knew that Christ had died on the cross for him. *Maybe God wants me to become a Christian,* he thought. *But how can I become a Christian in this communist camp? I am not free. I do not know who to ask about being a Christian.*

The major continued to think about his dream. *If God wants me to be a Christian, He will have to get me out of here,* he decided.

That evening for some reason the guard forgot to secure him in his stocks. A minor miracle! Although not bound, however, he was still a prisoner within the stockade.

Carefully he crept out to the perimeter and pushed gently against some of the stockade poles. Three in a row had been eaten off at the base by termites. They yielded just enough for him to worm his way under them. A second miracle!

As the fugitive started down the trail the communists saw him and gave chase with their guns blazing. As he ran he prayed that God would help him escape. It was almost as if he knew the trail, even though he had never been over it before. He managed to shake off his pursuers, but soon he was confronted by another obstacle—a river at flood stage.

The fleeing major knew there was no way he could wade across the swift waters. But he stepped in anyway and, as he did, another miracle took place. Everywhere he placed his foot it was as if there was a rock under it. He "walked" across that wild river on those "rocks."

The major finally reached the road to Pleiku and managed to hitchhike a ride back into town. Meanwhile, another part of the story was unfolding. When the major was reported missing, someone informed the Vietnamese pastor, who immediately went to see the major's Vietnamese wife. He told her the gospel story and promised to pray for her husband's safe return.

The woman was deeply into animism and spirit worship. Her house was known as an occult citadel, complete with sorcery paraphenalia.

"If my husband comes back here safely," she told the pastor, "I will believe there really is a God and give myself to Jesus."

When the major walked into his house unharmed, his wife told him the promise she had made.

"I think we both should follow Jesus," the man replied, remembering the vision he had seen. After declaring their faith in Christ, they had a huge bonfire in their front yard, burning up the trappings the woman had used to practice her sorcery.

That was just one of the many stories springing from the revival that swept through the highlands of Vietnam. Christians gathered early each morning to pray. God answered with signs and wonders and, most of all, with conversions.

Nor did the revival stop when South Vietnam fell and the communists took over. More about that later.

21

Cheo Reo

In telling God's love story of His mighty visitation at the 1971 National Church and Missionary Conferences and how the revival spread throughout the highlands, I got somewhat ahead of my story. We need, therefore, to go back to May, 1971 when the missionary conference took place.

EG and I had just come back to Vietnam from another stint at Dalat School in Malaysia. Should we return to Pleiku, or might there be an alternate location more conducive to Bible translation, which was by now more than ever my number one priority?

The rapid church growth, the constant casualties of war, the need to be a jack-of-all-trades, and changes in the Bible Society's requirements had hindered Rev. Sang's translation work. He and I agreed that I should pursue the project.

I was concerned that Pleiku, a provincial capital, was too busy. Not only did we have a very large church there, but there were large churches in the surrounding villages as well. Almost every day people would come to visit us or to ask us to help them in some way. Sometimes they would just drop by to say hello.

As much as I enjoyed all those things, I knew if I were going to finish the translation of the Jarai New Testament and Psalms I needed to be in a secluded place. If I stayed in Pleiku, I would often be saying "no," and people would not understand.

Cheo Reo, some 60 miles southeast of Pleiku, was also in the Jarai area. Like Pleiku, Cheo Reo had a strong central church. Like Pleiku, Cheo Reo was surrounded by Jarai villages. But Cheo Reo had fewer Jarai Christians in the surrounding villages and therefore fewer potential visitors.

I felt that Cheo Reo would afford me more of the solitude I needed. So at the missionary conference EG and I received permission to move to Cheo Reo.

The Mission-Church property in Cheo Reo was huge. Stately coconut palms lent a tropical aura to the place. The church was at the front of the property along the road. Behind the church was the pastor's residence, Still farther back was the house we would occupy. Behind our house was a small shed big enough for an electric generator and a few tools.

Our house was well situated, being somewhat isolated by the other buildings on the property. The one drawback was that there were numerous neighbors along the back fence line who had the habit of using our yard as a trash dump.

Cheo Reo was in a mountain-ringed basin about 600 feet above sea level. Compared with Pleiku, at 2,400 feet, it was hot. Some afternoons the thermometer in the kitchen would read 110 degrees before the stove was turned on! It was a little like living in a giant tea cup. There was normally no breeze whatsoever.

Storms had a habit of blowing back and forth across the valley. We would close the windows on one side of the house as the storm blew in. Then it would hit the mountains and bounce back, triggering a rush to close the windows on the other side.

The roads out of the valley were always dangerous. The narrow passes were perfect for ambushes. One afternoon I drove down through Red Mountain pass. A bulldozer operator was pushing the jungle back to eliminate hiding places for snipers. Later that evening I learned that a sniper had shot the operator right off the machine.

It was during this time that Franklin Irwin introduced Evangelism Deep and Wide to the Jarai. The basic building block of Evangelism Deep and Wide was cell groups. Christians would share their faith with friends and neighbors and soon an informal group would start. Once a cell grew to 16 people, it divided, each cell continuing to witness and evangelize.

Those cell groups may have saved the Vietnamese Church. When the communists came in, bent on destroying the Church, the Christians were able to function effectively without the congregation having to gather at a central meeting place. Each of the cell groups was its own support system, encouraging the believers and winning the unconverted—a mini-Church.

The growth of the total Church in the highlands of Vietnam under communist occupation is one of

the brightest stories in the annals of Christianity.
The cell group concept of Evangelism Deep and
Wide helped make it possible. I hope that someday
the story can be told in full.

The revival, by then widespread, although
primarily in the tribal highlands, also served to
wean Christians from dependence on Western and
Vietnamese missionaries. We had practiced ac-
countability to the Jarai pastors. This prepared
them to be at the front of the revival and its great
future. Although we did not know it then, the
cataclysmic events of March and April 1975 were
not that far off.

When EG and I first moved to Cheo Reo the
Jarai consulted me about many things, including
evangelism plans and Church problems. I was not
asking for a leadership role, but out of love and
respect they included me in practically everything.
I knew they had been doing well without me and
yet we all enjoyed the fellowship. We were all
facing death as a way of life for the sake of the
gospel. That bond tied us together.

Through a most amazing and unexpected experience God removed leadership responsibility
from me in a moment.

The revival-inspired prayer meetings were already
in full swing in Cheo Reo. Our house was only 50
yards from the church and when the people were
all praying audibly we could hear the buzz—like
bees in a hive.

A few weeks after the Holy Spirit fired up the
Cheo Reo revival I entered the church through a
side door that put me about even with the pulpit.

The sanctuary was filled with people. Many were on their knees. Some were prostrate on the floor. All were praying with all their might.

As I stood there observing and listening, it was as if the Lord walked in that door behind me. I sensed His presence, although I did not see anyone. And then it was as if He reached out and lifted the Jarai out of my hands and passed them to those in the church. The burden was gone—the burden to preach to them, the burden to lead the efforts to evangelize them.

Instinctively I knew it was final. God was relieving me of all those concerns.

It was so real that I turned around and walked back home. This was their revival. I was simply an observer. It was as if I had left the Heavenly Visitor in the church with the Jarai. I was no longer at the center of things. I was somewhere on the periphery.

It was awesome to sense and to see God's love for the Jarai.

But I also knew I had one final responsibility—to complete the New Testament and Psalms in Jarai.

I redoubled my efforts to finish the job.

22

Joy in His Presence

Every day I worked with my two consultants, Wing and Blo. Of course, we had numerous translation helps, including all the English translations of the New Testament, Greek references and other books.

Apart from my daily hours with Wing and Blo and, of course, with EG, I practically became a hermit. All my life I had been a people person. I love to talk! And there was never a limit to the number of people anxious to sharpen their English by conversing with the American missionary.

Fortunately the Cheo Reo pastor was a willing accomplice to protect me from the public. He wanted the New Testament in Jarai and he knew that interruptions would only delay its completion. He wanted me to keep on working.

Almost daily he asked me, "Where is the Book?" When people came by wanting to see me he would stop them at the gate and explain that I was busy.

One caller, however, managed to slip by the pastor's protective screen. I was in an intense translating session with Wing and Blo when the knock came at my door.

"*Hoget ih kiang?* (What do you want?)" I asked gruffly of the slight Jarai teenager standing before me. My manner was both culturally inappropriate and un-Christlike.

The youth lifted the camouflage military cap from his head, removed his dark sunglasses and said timidly, "I have heard that you help people with leprosy here. Will you help me?" Signs of the disease furrowed his young face.

Instantly the words of Jesus zapped me: "Whatever you did for one of the least of these brothers of mine, you did for me" (Matthew 25:40). Ashamed of myself for my irritation and rudeness, I gave the boy bus fare to the Pleiku Leprosy Center.

Within a month he was back. At the Center he had received Jesus Christ as his Savior and had brought five of his friends to Christ. For me it was a serious lesson. Being Christlike can take no holidays—not even to translate the Holy Scriptures!

✦ ✦ ✦

Within sight of where my informants and I worked the rusting remains of a fire-charred motorbike reminded me that time was short. The bike had belonged to the church's former pastor, Ama Tum, a man well-known to me from our years together in Pleiku.

Pastor Tum was a true man of God, one of those sweet, loving, angelic sorts. He had a ready smile and a humble, tender spirit. If he had any faults I was not aware of them. He was far ahead of me in spiritual development and in his walk with the Lord.

One of my earliest memories of Ama Tum went back several years to when he was beginning his Pleiku ministry. He had approached me with a question.

"Oi Dlong," he asked, "what should I do? When I go out to preach they laugh at me."

"They laugh at me, too," I responded quickly. "I'm six-feet-four, a foreigner and ugly. But, do you know, Jesus called me to serve Him and I have plenty of seed to sow. I am going to sow and sow and sow the seed, no matter how much people laugh.

"Jesus has given you seed to sow, too," I continued. "And some day, if you and I sow enough seed, someone is going to reap a harvest. Somewhere there will be a great harvest. You and I may never see it. But I am willing to sow the seed so that some day someone else will reap a harvest. What about you?"

Ama Tum gave me a big, wonderful smile.

"I understand," he said. And evidently he did, for he personally won about 200 people to Christ as he ministered to his fellow Jarai.

One day Ama Tum went to a village south of Cheo Reo to preach. The villagers told me that as he began the trip home on his motorbike they heard gun shots. They looked and saw that the pastor, now standing by his bike, was surrounded by men in black—Viet Cong.

One of the rounds evidently hit the pastor's hand,

for he was holding it as though in pain. There, at point blank range, the communists shot Pastor Tum in the chest and set fire to his motorbike.

Pastor Tum left a widow and seven children.

When the communists tortured and killed Ga Hao, the Pleiku pastor, years earlier, I was angry. Why would a sovereign God allow such a senseless, misguided act?

When they shot Pastor Tan at Le Thanh in 1965 and tossed his body by the side of the road like so much garbage, I was again angry.

But through the martyrdom of Ama Tum, I finally came to understand that those like Stephen (Acts 7) who die for their Christian testimony have a special place in heaven forever.

Selfishly I had wanted Ga Hao and Pastor Tan back on earth in the dirt, pain, sickness, trouble and misery of war-torn Vietnam. But God had provided them something infinitely better. He was filling them—and Ama Tum—"with joy in [His] presence, with eternal pleasures at [His] right hand" (Psalm 16:11).

All the time I was in Cheo Reo, Ama Tum's charred and rusting bike standing under the shed just behind our house was a constant reminder to me that my commitment to the gospel needed to be as total as his—and that time was fast running out.

23

The Apostle Paul Speaks Jarai

We were in Cheo Reo when the communists mounted their 1972 offensive. More accurately, I was in Cheo Reo. EG was at the Dalat School in Malaysia helping combat an outbreak of hepatitis.

With many of the South Vietnamese communists having been discovered and dispatched in the ill-fated 1968 Tet offensive, this was essentially an offensive from the North. My two translation helpers, Wing and Blo, were alarmed.

"This is really big," they exclaimed. "The communists have tanks this time. We don't know what's going to happen. We must go to our families."

Under the circumstances I felt that it was a reasonable request. So they left for their villages with my blessing. But now I had no translators.

By this time most of the big American military units had been withdrawn from Vietnam. There were only seven or eight Americans still in Cheo Reo. I did not know what to expect.

Rumor had it that the North Vietnamese might

come in on Highway 19 from Cambodia and cut the country in half. If that happened, the dividing line would be through either Pleiku or Cheo Reo.

I made up a "ditty" bag: a mosquito net, malaria pills and various essentials should I need to go hide in one of the villages. By this time I was determined to finish the Jarai New Testament—even if it cost my life.

In one sense, I found it hard to proceed without the input of my helpers. But the revival the year before had profoundly affected me. My prayer life was on a very keen edge. I found great delight in plumbing the depths of God's written Word, seeking to put it into good Jarai and relying on the Holy Spirit to be my Helper.

We had freshly translated the largely narrative Gospels and the Acts. We had also completed Romans, quite a different style of writing. But I was not satisfied with Romans. It was too word-for-word, too wooden. I asked God to help me make it "speak Jarai."

So, with no wife and no helpers, I set to work alone. I did not pay attention to day or night. I did not pay attention to meal times. I would sometimes still be at work at three o'clock in the morning. And if I felt sleepy at 10 o'clock I would lie down and take a nap. It was just the Lord and me and the book of Romans.

That became my schedule 24 hours a day for probably close to six weeks. I lost track of clock and calendar, so absorbed was I in the work. It was a wonderful experience of being bathed in the presence of God, communing with Him in two or three languages.

Finally the translation of Romans was complete. I typed it in triplicate and gave it to three readers, along with a critiquing system. If a sentence or verse was not good Jarai, they would put a certain number beside it. If the grammar was poor they would mark it with another number. If a word was misspelled the word itself would get still another number.

The first reader appeared back at my door in record time. I was surprised to see him because he had had the manuscript only a few days. It was rolled tightly as he held it before him. The outer page looked dirty and worn from much handling.

"Oi Dlong," the man began, tears welling in his eyes, "this book is wonderful, especially chapters six, seven and eight. Can I have a copy?"

I had received other manuscripts with technical comments but this one came back wrung in a man's hands. By this time tears were running down his face. Instinctively I knew this translation of Romans "spoke Jarai."

✦ ✦ ✦

The 1972 communist offensive collapsed and South Vietnam still stood, although the threat of more trouble was never far away. The hepatitis emergency at Dalat School lifted and EG and Joby rejoined me in Cheo Reo.

Wing and Blo also returned, reporting that the mighty revival was continuing to spread.

"Oi," Blo announced very matter-of-factly, "I've been filled with the Holy Spirit." What a story followed!

Blo, along with some other believers, was at the church for a prayer meeting one night. Suddenly people came running to the building.

"What do you want?" those who were praying asked.

"We've come to put out the fire!" responded the villagers.

The fire, the believers soon found out, was an observable glow suspended over the church. The non-Christians thought the building was on fire—and in a sense it was. All the churches were on fire.

We pressed on with the New Testament translation amid threat of instant annihilation. Our Mission headquarters sent a letter to all families in the more dangerous areas of Vietnam, offering wives the option of evacuating to Bangkok.

As EG read the letter she turned and put her arms around my waist.

"Honey," she said, her eyes glistening, "I will go anywhere in the world with you and nowhere without you!"

Discussion over!

✦ ✦ ✦

About a hundred yards from our house there was a military base. Intermittently the communists would fire mortar rounds at the base. Some of the shots fell very close to our house. When it comes to mortars, a hundred yards is not a very big margin.

Whenever a barrage started, I would grab Joby, about five at the time, and we would all run down the outside stairs to a ground-level room where we had a mattress on the cement floor, two rows of 55-gallon steel drums for protection and a fan to alleviate the heat. An American sergeant gave us a PR-90 army radio with their weekly frequencies so we could at least be warned of danger. We heard a lot of battle talk but never had to use our code word for help: Man in Black.

Never before or since was I so afraid for my children. For some reason I imagined Joby maimed with a lost eye or leg. In all the previous years in Vietnam I had never had that kind of fear. Fortunately I managed to conceal it in front of EG and Joby. It was not until many years later that I shared my fear with EG.

By 1973 all the American combat units were gone. The military situation was visibly deteriorating on a daily basis. But the revival in Cheo Reo was intensifying. It was marked by mass prayer meetings and a willingness on the part of Christians to tell others about Jesus Christ.

Every Sunday afternoon four or five teams of believers went out, each team visiting three villages. That meant that 12 to 15 villages were hearing the gospel every Sunday.

Sunday evenings they would gather back at the church to report what had happened. Never had there been such a concentrated evangelistic effort in the Cheo Reo valley. Churches were springing up everywhere.

And while the Jarai Christians were building the Church of Jesus Christ I was preparing a translation of God's Word for the use of that Church.

What a partnership!

24

Not a Moment Too Soon

Picture the scene, if you will: three men surrounding an eight-and-a-half-inch tall by six-and-a-half-inch wide stapled notebook about a quarter of an inch thick. The cover pictures a Vietnamese scene with water buffaloes, banana trees and "Sunrise" printed across its cover.

Wing, a young Jarai high school graduate sits poised with his Bic pen, the notebook and a Vietnamese Bible which was translated by Mrs. Grace Hazenberg Cadman, who held a M.A. in classical languages, and the Rev. John Olsen. Although Mrs. Cadman's name always sounded ancient, like Tyndale or Wycliffe, in reality she had been a missionary to Vietnam only a few decades before me.

Blo is sitting on Wing's right. He is usually quiet as he thumbs through the Raday New Testament translated by Bob Ziemer. I sit on Wing's left and have at least a half dozen books open before me and piles of references within easy reach.

What you have just "seen" is the Jarai Bible translation team at work.

We always began the translating sessions with prayer that God would speak to Jarai readers as He had to the earliest readers of the Bible in the original languages. I would then read a verse and think it through out loud. Sometimes the Jarai ran a close parallel to the original, since adjectives followed the nouns they modified, just like Greek.

Wing, always quick of mind and speech, was eager to get it on paper.

Blo always made sure that it was simple and practical so that the men in the village could understand.

We laughed. We cried. We cheered. We groaned.

"Puh, puh, puh, puh!" As Wing transcribed the translation he pursed and popped his lips as if he were dry spitting. Wing and Blo especially got into the stories of Jesus and the disciples. When Jesus turned to the disciples in the boat on the Sea of Galilee and asked, "Why are you frightened? Are you still without faith?" the wind would sigh out of Wing and Blo. They would click their tongues, shake their heads and say, "Oh, what a shame for the poor disciples!"

Sometimes it took a whole morning to complete one verse. Sometimes we sailed through many verses with ease.

We always broke at noon for lunch. As soon as they were out the door I would start banging out the morning's work on the typewriter in triplicate for the readers to check.

One day, an American soldier noticed that I was using carbon paper. A few days later he returned with a big box of computer paper, five-colored rolls with carbon paper between each layer, all lined up. The five copies easily separated into same color piles for distribution to readers. It was a gift from heaven!

The next step was to bring the work to a committee of Jarai to read and critique together. After this grilling, I would retype the manuscript and give it to other readers who also sent back their findings. Slowly and painfully each book took its final form.

A large sign at the Pleiku Air Force Base said it in big, bold letters: Zero Defects. That was our goal—a dynamic translation and a perfect typesetting.

Besides the Jarai New Testament and Psalms, we had a second project that was absorbing much of EG's attention. Back in the early 1950s, Grady and Evelyn Mangham, the first missionaries to work among the Jarai, had prepared and published a Jarai hymnal which contained 72 English songs they had translated.

In Vietnam, as in most third world countries, churches do not provide hymnals in the pews. People buy their own and carry them to and from church along with their Bibles. These now-aging Jarai hymnals were cherished by the Christians, but they were literally disintegrating.

The believers begged us to prepare a new hymnal for them. EG responded to the challenge by translating another 200 hymns and songs. We wanted the Jarai to supply indigenous tunes for at least some of these hymns, but the people flatly refused.

"No, Oi, Ya," they said, "our own music is wicked. The words are about worshiping spirits, about illicit sex, about things we won't have any part of today. The old music brings back the old words. We want to use your music with Jarai words."

So even though we had tried to make a cultural transition, the Christians wanted none of it. Now this new hymnal for the Jarai was also in the final stages of preparation and could soon go to press.

✦ ✦ ✦

"Joby has been on a spree for two or three weeks talking about Grand-mama and Grand-daddy," our letter home began. "She wants to know what kind of plane will take us to your house, who will meet us, what kind of house we'll live in. You'd think she is ready for furlough!

"Our hot season is moving in on us and already we are feeling it. Can't imagine what it's going to be like in June, July and August! We've decided the climate here is like six to eight months of July and the rest like May and June. Joby comes in every afternoon and turns the tub full of water and plays in it to cool off. Does Grand-daddy have any bubble bath?"

I was alone in Cheo Reo as I wrote my folks in the spring of 1972.

My heart breaks as I contemplate what could happen to thousands, even millions, of South Vietnamese this year. Some don't deserve liberty. They have cheated, stolen or otherwise not contributed to their country, but millions have given everything to keep from having communism.

I can't face running, but my reason tells me it'll be very bad for me and all my friends in the church. Pray that God will again intervene and spare the nation. These past few days I have suddenly realized how much I enjoy living and my wife and my family and that I wouldn't mind living a few more years at all.

The next day I received a cable:

National church requests worldwide Alliance unite fasting prayer May seventh for Vietnam solution. A cable has been sent to all Mission chairmen around the world asking that they share this request with church leaders and missionaries in each country. Doubtless, you will want to set that day aside especially to pray with our brethren in Vietnam. Missionary Personnel: Everyone is reported safe and in good spirits. The word from Mr. Stebbins is, "Morale is very high."

A week or so later I wrote my folks again:

I am working hard during the week from 7 a.m. to 10 or 10:30 p.m. on the translation. We are up through John and should finish the book by the end of May. That leaves Acts and Psalms to do. I spent several hours typing this morning. Then I cleaned up the house from three weeks of bachelor living.

Tomorrow I am to preach at the Vietnamese church. Last Sunday I preached in the Jarai church. Also on Sundays at 11 a.m. I have a Bible study for the few American advisors (only 12) that are stationed here.

There is the chance that an attack on Cheo Reo is coming from just north of town. In choosing to stay, two passages from Galatians guided me: (1) I was chosen before I was born; (2) I have died already with Christ and the life that I now live is His. Also He gives the gold (the parable of the talents) and we choose how best to invest it. I felt that I could accomplish nothing away from here alone, whereas here with Wing and Blo we can sometimes do 50 verses a day. I don't want to have to run, but my bags are packed should I have to go. Surely the Lord will give us enough months to finish the translation.

Then a couple of weeks later:

Surprise! I had two letters today, one from each of you. I flew to Saigon May 18 to work on the new Jarai hymnbook and ran into all kinds of surprises. I had to audit Mission books and was asked to stay and meet the executive committee the following Wednesday.

We have been asked to take the Saigon Church again while we do our translation work there. The Sunday service is on Armed

Forces Radio throughout Vietnam. Then, a unanimous, urgent request from the Dalat School came for us to return there for one year to be girls' dorm parents. The school loses 15 to furlough and headquarters has only one replacement.

Also, about the same time, a telegram came from headquarters saying that if we had to evacuate Vietnam, for us to take the Bangkok English church. EG said that when she decided to be a missionary she thought that was her last decision!

Here is what has been decided, and we have asked the Lord to close it if He has something different in mind. I am packing to go to Saigon now. Wing will go with me. My first Sunday service is June 11. EG will go back to Malaysia with the kids to be dorm parent and I will go as soon as I can, probably middle of August.

The school will allow me to have a vow not to shave until the translation is finished. They wanted me to shave to take the Saigon church and I told them they really didn't want me, to get someone else. Now they will take me beard and all. I'll have to send you a picture. It is a good reminder that the translation must be done.

I hated to have to tell the people here that I am leaving, but they seemed to think it a good thing. Kontum is under heavy pressure and just south of us there is lots of fighting. There was a terrible earthquake here Tuesday. Sunday the pastor read from Matthew 24. He warned the Church that the Lord could come soon.

When I came to Vietnam, of the 28 tribes there were Christians in less than 10. Now there are Christians in all 28 tribal groups. We have had over 50 new believers since January 1 and many people are listening to us now who would not listen before.

Once I was at the school in Penang I set a grueling schedule for myself. During the day, while the kids were in classes, I worked on the manuscript, retyping it so that it was absolutely correct, making sure the section heads were in place, the proper names capitalized, the quotation marks where they belonged. It was tedious, technical work.

When classes recessed in the afternoon, I made myself available to the kids until their bedtime and it was usually close to midnight before I crawled in myself. I calculated that I was working about 90 hours each week.

In the midst of it, as might be predicted, I became desperately ill. I had terrible stomach pains and cramps, along with diarrhea. I was taken to the local Seventh Day Adventist hospital and subjected to a battery of tests, none of which pinpointed any organic problem. The doctors were baffled.

I, too, was baffled—and frustrated.

"Lord," I prayed as I lay flat on my back in that hospital room, "why do I have to be here in this hospital? What have I done to displease You, Lord? I should be working on the manuscript. I should be with the kids. The school doesn't have the luxury of extra staff people who can substitute. I came all the way from Vietnam to work with these kids and here I am in the hospital. All the responsibility I should be sharing has fallen on my wife and Nurse Joy [Boese]."

As I searched my heart and talked to God, the Lord brought me to Isaiah 40:11: "He shall feed his flock like a shepherd: he shall gather the lambs with his arm, and carry them in his bosom, and shall gently lead those that are with young." (KJV)

Suddenly I saw myself as a skittish little lamb. Ever since I had become a Christian in 1953 at age 18, I had been busy serving God, bouncing all over the pasture, doing what I thought God wanted me to do—preaching and teaching and accomplishing what I considered to be His work and His will.

But God let me know that I had not given Him—the Shepherd—time to love me as a little lamb. I cannot describe the awful, awful shame I felt. I was speechless. My ears burned. I pulled the bedsheet up over my head to hide from God. I realized that even a pet dog has the sense to go to its master and let him stroke its head and show it affection. And I was so busy running around doing God's work that I had not taken time to let God gather me in His arms like a lamb and to carry me close to His heart.

In that moment, I yielded myself to God.

"Lord," I continued, "I am very ashamed of myself. Please forgive me. I have been insensitive to You, my Master."

As I prayed, it was as if God was stroking me like a shepherd might stroke a lamb. I have not had a

sensation like it before nor since. On the one hand
I felt ashamed and, on the other, loved and
cherished by the Eternal God.

Later that afternoon my doctor stepped into the
room.

"Doctor," I greeted him, "I know what's the matter with me!"

"You do?" he asked quizically.

"Yes, let me read it to you." I took out the writing
tablet on which I had recorded what had transpired
between me and God.

When I finished reading, a most unexpected
thing happened: The doctor fell on his knees beside
my bed.

"Pray for me!" he cried.

As we prayed I realized that I was witnessing an
extension of the reality that was sweeping through
South Vietnam in those years—the reality of the
revival—touching the hearts of missionaries, Vietnamese and tribespeople, Christian and non-Chris-
tian.

Those days in the hospital and the weeks that followed were a time of very deep personal relationship with God—an experience that continues to
affect my walk with Him to this day.

❖   ❖   ❖

Our four-year term was up in July 1973 and we
were looking forward to furlough for two reasons—
both my mother and grandmother were facing
surgery and uncertain futures. I wanted to be near
them at this crisis time in their lives.

But as we prayed for wisdom we decided that the
New Testament and the hymnal were too urgent to
wait another two years—one year of furlough and
another year for typesetting. We determined to
trust God to preserve the lives of our loved ones if
it was His will that we see them again on earth.

We requested a one-year extension to our term
and the Mission granted our request. The way was
now clear for us to see our projects through to the
end.

It was not a moment too soon!

25

Saigon Wrap-Up

Everywhere, it seemed, God's Spirit was at work in unusual ways and with unusual response to the preaching of the Word and the faithful witness of believers. The fire was continuing to spread.

During the school vacation, Nathan, Eddie and I returned to Vietnam to finish up some translation work. The weekdays were occupied with lots of sweat and just plain hard work, but Sundays were glorious as I had the opportunity to preach in five different locations.

The Pleiku church was packed. The aisles and the back were filled, with many people standing outside. There was a sea of new faces, new believers—600 of them in the first six months of 1972. The church had consistently sent out witness bands each Sunday afternoon and they had reaped a bountiful harvest.

The second Sunday I preached to a full church at an all-Christian village near Pleiku. They had already established one other church of 50 believers, and other small groups were meeting in many villages nearby.

The third Sunday I was invited to preach and share the Lord's Supper with the 200 Christian refugees at the Pleiku Leprosy Treatment Center. We had only 30 communion glasses so we had to refill them several times.

The fourth Sunday I preached at Cheo Reo where the problem now was whether to take out the front or the back wall to accommodate the overflow crowds. There were also many new believers in the villages around Cheo Reo. One thousand people had been lead to Christ by the lay people of the church in the year since I had left. After years of sowing, it was now harvest time.

The fifth Sunday I spoke to the staff and students of the Nhatrang Theological Seminary. The joy of the Lord was evident in the congregation as the director welcomed us warmly.

✦ ✦ ✦

During the extended year for finishing up the translation project, our base became Saigon. It was imperative that we be where we could easily make contact with the typesetters and printers. The house normally occupied by Tom and Donna Stebbins was empty while they were in the States on furlough. So we set up shop in the Stebbins' home.

We slept in one of the two bedrooms and installed two large tables in the other—one table for me and the Jarai New Testament and one for EG and the Jarai hymnal. Our children were all in school in Malaysia, safely out of Vietnam's deterioriating military and political situation.

I would rise each morning at five o'clock, long before daylight, and jog for three miles around an oval track near our home. I chose to run in the pre-dawn hours for two reasons: one, the heat in always-hot and humid Saigon is least intense at that hour and, two, the pollution from the glut of motor bikes and other two-cycle-engined vehicles is lower. Even so, I would return home and my saliva would be black.

As I jogged, I prayed. I prayed for Vietnam, Cambodia and Laos. I prayed that somehow God would Himself live in the minds and hearts of the people. I remember looking up at the stars and pleading with God to send great waves of salvation over the people in all three lands.

Back again at the house, I made myself a tall glass of honey-sweetened iced tea and set about to have my devotions. Because I was working so closely with the New Testament and all the technicalities involved in its translation and printing, I chose to use the Old Testament for my devotions. The insights I noted in the margins were thrilling. What an experience it was to be totally immersed in God's Word almost every waking hour.

Then EG would wake up and we would have breakfast together. We worked every morning until lunch time. Following lunch we took a catnap and then went back to work, sometimes until ten or eleven at night. It was a wonderful time, both of us involved in projects intended for the long-range building of the Jarai Church.

For some diversion, we would get on our little 50 CC Yamaha motorbike and scoot around town.

The traffic was always heavy and often scary. If another vehicle came a little too close, EG would hang on even tighter. Thankfully, we survived unscathed.

We always looked forward to Monday evenings, when the Saigon missionary corps gathered for prayer and fellowship. We saw many answers to our prayers, including one that impacted the printing of the new Jarai hymnal.

A man in North Carolina had reminded my mother that if we ever needed money she should let him know. So I wrote Mom to tell the man that we needed $2,000 for printing paper which would be stored until presstime six or eight months later. With inflation spiraling, we were advised to buy as soon as possible.

The following Sunday at church a friend met me at the door and handed me a check.

"Here, Charlie," he said, "I want to help you with your hymnbook." It was a check for $250.

That meant we would have $2,250 for paper. But when the check arrived from America, it was not for $2,000 but for $3,000, making a total of $3,250. I was shaken. Had I mistakenly put down $3,000 instead of $2,000 when I wrote my mother?

We went ahead and bought the paper and put it in the Mission warehouse. When we got the bill the total was $3,240. I was stunned.

I walked out of the building, sat down on my motorbike, put my helmet on, raised my hand to heaven and with a slight smile on my face said, "Lord, You knew all the time, didn't You?"

By the time the hymnal went to press the paper

would have cost us $6,000.

The hymnal came off the press in June 1974. Gail Fleming hauled the books up to Pleiku. Within one month the entire first printing of 5,000 copies was sold out.

Two weeks before our July furlough we finished the New Testament and Psalms. The graphics were done and all 810 pages of text were typeset, proofed and ready for printing by the United Bible Societies in Hong Kong.

✦ ✦ ✦

You might say Oi Wao (Uh-ee WOW) was the capstone of my missionary career. Oi Wao was an elderly man who lived near Pleiku. He had leprosy.

I had known him for 14 years and all that time I had witnessed to him about Jesus Christ. But he always rejected the gospel.

In May 1974 I made one final flying trip up to Pleiku to retrieve some last-minute pages of translation from Pastor Sang. The errand completed, I was scheduled to fly back to Saigon the next afternoon.

But all that day and night Oi Wao was on my mind. I even woke up in the middle of the night thinking about him. And every time I thought about him I prayed for him.

I can't leave Pleiku without seeing Oi Wao, I decided.

Morning dawned rainy and wet, not the best of weather for a 30-mile trip over poor roads. I had to see Oi Wao.

I borrowed the leprosarium's pickup, loaded some Jarai young people from the high school onto the truck bed and headed to Oi Wao's village.

When we reached the outskirts of the town I asked, "Is Oi Wao still living? Is he around?"

"Oh, yes. He's still living," the villagers replied, "but he is very old now. He's out in the woods tying up his horse. He'll be back soon."

We waited.

Finally Oi Wao appeared, walking somewhat slowly with the help of a long cane. As he approached I noticed that cataracts clouded his eyes. I was afraid he would not be able to see me.

"Oi Wao!" I called while he was still at a distance. "Do you remember me? I'm Oi Long!"

"I remember you, Oi Long," the old man responded with a grin. "Let me sit down here. I must be the oldest Jarai living. I must be 130 years old. All the Jarai I've known are dead by now!" Despite the rain and mud, he haunched down in typical tribal posture. I squatted beside him.

"Oi Wao," I began, "some day I'm going to go to heaven. When I get to heaven I want you to be there, too. I've told you about Jesus over and over."

"I know you have," the old man replied. "I want to see you there in heaven. I want Jesus in my heart!"

I could hardly believe my ears! Right there in the rain, with 100 or more villagers and the Jarai high school students looking on, I prayed with Oi Wao as he received Christ into his life.

I was on cloud nine!

The students and I got into the pickup and drove back to the mission.

"I need to get to the airport," I called to Ama Tet (Aa-maa TET) as we drove through the gate. "But

Oi Wao just prayed this morning to receive Christ. Will you follow him up?"

That was the last event of my missionary career in Pleiku, the highland town where EG and I had first put down roots in South Vietnam, where we had learned the Jarai language, where we had ministered for more than two terms, where we had begun the arduous task of translating the Jarai New Testament.

Somehow Oi Wao tied it all together—the hard work, the high risk, the discouraging fruitlessness turned around by God-sent revival, the bittersweet future of the Jarai tribespeople, pressed cruelly by alien overlords.

And the reaping and the still reaping of a thousandfold highland harvest.

✦ ✦ ✦

"Would you do it again?" you may ask.

Do you mean would I fall in love with EG again?

Do you mean would I receive the love of Jesus Christ into my heart and life again?

Do you mean would I take that love to the Montagnards of Vietnam?

I have only to see in my mind's eye the face of Oi Wao that morning, his cataract-clouded eyes somehow bright in the new spiritual knowledge of sins forgiven, to know it was worth it.

✦ ✦ ✦

In February 1975 the printed Word of God reached the Jarai.

Less than three weeks later, all missionaries were forced from the Jarai area by the deteriorating military situation.

And on April 30, 1975, South Vietnam capitulated.

The dark shroud of communism now enveloped all of Vietnam.

In North Carolina, far from the turmoil, EG and I agonized. We knew that all but seven Western missionaries had now been safely evacuated. Tom Stebbins had been on one of the last helicopter shuttles from atop the American embassy.

We also knew that some of our Christians were among the tens of thousands of Vietnamese and tribespeople who also escaped the communist takeover. Yet others would be among the "boat people" who followed.

We were also profoundly thankful that even though the Jarai might be entering a long, dark night, they would enter it singing the hymns EG had put in permanent form. And they would enter it with the instruction and comfort of the Holy Scriptures I had helped to translate and publish.

EG and I had run our race against time and, with God's help, we had won!

✦ ✦ ✦

Charlie loves EG!
EG loves Charlie!
Jesus loves Charlie!
Charlie loves Jesus!
God loves the Jarai!
The Jarai love God!

Epilogue

We do not want you to be uninformed,
brothers, about the hardships we suffered in
the province of Asia. We were under great
pressure, far beyond our ability to endure,
so that we despaired even of life.
   Indeed, in our hearts we felt the sentence
of death. But this happened that we might
not rely on ourselves but on God, who raises
the dead. . . .
   He has delivered us from such a deadly
peril, and he will deliver us. On him we have
set our hope that he will continue to deliver
us, as you help us by your prayers. Then
many will give thanks on our behalf for the
gracious favor granted us in answer to the
prayers of many. (2 Corinthians 1:8-9, 11)

Any epilogue to these three love stories could be much larger than the stories themselves. In the spring of 1975 we were hesitant, but planning to return to Vietnam even though we felt that the country would fall. The final battle of March and April was a nightmare for anyone with friends in Vietnam.

To the glory of God, the Jarai New Testament was dedicated and presented to the Jarai people at the Pleiku Church on February 16, 1975. Many sent letters describing the joy of that day and expressing regret that we were not there. According to their accounts many of the books were quickly taken and in use when one month later, on March 9, the assault began at Banmethuout that would end in the abandonment of the highlands and the fall of Vietnam.

Richard and Lillian Phillips, Norman and Joan Johnson and Betty Mitchell were captured at Banmethuout. I jogged and prayed for them during two missionary tours.

One day as I jogged past a cornfield in Dayton, Ohio I felt the burden lift. I knew they were free. The news came later on the television that they had been released in Hanoi. It was October, 1975.

When the Saigon government decided to remove its forces from Pleiku, 100,000 Vietnamese, who had fled to Pleiku as the communists advanced, headed down through the Cheo Reo valley. Only about 1,000 actually made it to the coast.

The Montagnards, of all the tribes, did not leave their homes in the highlands, but there was a news blackout about their fate. I prayed for them but resisted the temptation to write anyone, for fear the contact would cause them hardship.

The blackout lasted 10 years.

Then, in 1985, 200 Montagnard crossed the Cambodia/Thai border. At last we had news!

When the North Vietnamese conquered the highlands, the refugees reported, they began an intense campaign of interrogation, imprisonment, beatings and fearful mistreatment of the tribespeople. Many fled to the jungle where they were finally able to assemble.

Five tribes—Koho, Mnong, Raday, Jarai and Bahnar—united to form Dega (Day GAA)—Mountain Nation. Raday became their official language and they established a government with offices and branches like the former Vietnamese government. All efforts to get other nations to recognize them failed.

The Dega mustered an army of 30,000 men and controlled the highland jungles for a time. Each dry season the new communist government would send several divisions of troops to destroy them.

The great revival of 1971 continued and the Dega became Christians by the thousands. Forced by the seizure of their churches and prohibited from assembly, they learned to meet in small groups and to pray. Many miracles accompanied their gatherings.

Pol Pot of Cambodia befriended the 200 Dega who had escaped to Thailand. They were moved by the U.S. to a refugee camp in the Philippines. Our congregation at North Ridge Alliance in Raleigh gave EG and me leave to go there to teach them for a month, as part of their English language and cultural training before they were brought to the States.

What an awesome experience it was to sing from the hymnal and preach from the Bible we had worked so long and hard to finish 11 years before.

✦ ✦ ✦

A few Jarai have trickled out of Vietnam. Each brings news of miracles and of extensive Jarai church growth. The numbers expanded from 7,000 in 1975 to 13,000 by 1985, then 27,000.

A 35-year-old deaf and dumb man well known to the community was healed and given God's Word to preach. The miracle was so great and his preaching so powerful that the Holy Spirit used him to add 13,000 to the Church. "The deaf and dumb preaches!" they said.

In 1972 there were about 53,000 Christian and Missionary Alliance baptized church members in Vietnam. In 1992, the number reached more than 248,000—62,000 of them being Jarai believers.

Thy kingdom come, thy will be done on earth as it is in heaven.

✦   ✦   ✦

The Longs currently serve the North Ridge Alliance Church in Raleigh, North Carolina.

John Nathan married Peggy Young, a nurse. He is the director of a heart catherization laboratory in Pinehurst, North Carolina. They have two boys, Steven and Jordan and one girl, Kristen.

Robert Edward (Eddie) married Kathy Christiansen whom he met at Crown College. Ed is a building superintendent in Raleigh, North Carolina and a deacon at the North Ridge Church. They have three girls—Lacey, Anna and Bethany.

Amelia Susan (Susie) graduated from Toccoa Falls College and earned her nursing degree. She is a missionary at Dalat School.

Joanna Elizabeth (Joby) graduated from Crown

College and married Mark Mitchell. They back-packed around the world, visiting numerous mission fields and assisting in various ways. They live and work in Coeur d'Alene, Idaho, preparing for graduate studies.